LEARN TO

INVEST

KAI L. WOOD

LEARN TO INVEST

Like the great investors

First edition: September 2024

Copyright ©2024 Kai L. Wood

All rights reserved. The partial or total reproduction of this work by any means or procedure, including reprography and digital processing, as well as the distribution of copies through rental or public lending, is strictly prohibited without the written authorization of the copyright holders, under the sanctions established by law.

TABLE OF CONTENTS

Introduction 7

The importance of investing 11
    Introduction to investing 11
    Why investing is crucial 24
    Basic investment principles 30
    Types of investments 40

Investment strategies 59
    Value investing 59
    Growth investing 60
    Dividend investing 62
    Passive investing 64

Legendary investors and their strategies 67
    Warren Buffett: the oracle of Omaha 67
    Joel Greenblatt: the little book that beats the market 74
    Michael Burry: the visionary of the great recession 81
    Peter Lynch: investing in what you know 88
    Ray Dalio: principles and bridgewater approach 94
    Benjamin Graham: the father of value investing 101
    John Bogle: the pioneer of indexed investing 107
    Bill Ackman: activism and persuasion 113
    Stanley Druckenmiller: macro and markets 119
    Geraldine Weiss: the dividend lady 125

Epilogue 131

INTRODUCTION

In a world where the global economy moves at a dizzying pace and the value of money erodes over time, investing is no longer an option but a necessity. Beyond simply being a means of generating wealth, investing has become an indispensable tool for protecting the future, ensuring economic stability, and achieving the much-desired financial independence. However, for many, the path to investing can seem like an intimidating labyrinth, full of complex decisions and considerable risks. So, how can one, without being an expert, find the right way in this vast and sometimes overwhelming financial universe?

This book has been created precisely to guide you through that journey. It is not just a compilation of financial theories but a compendium of practical and accessible wisdom, based on the proven strategies of the most successful investors in the world. Throughout these pages, you will not only learn the essential fundamentals of investing but also delve into the brilliant minds that have mastered this art, discovering how they have built fortunes and left a lasting legacy in the financial world.

The first step on this journey is to understand why investing is a cornerstone of wealth building. Throughout history, from the earliest civilizations to today, humanity has sought ways to grow its assets. In today's world, with the constant threat of inflation, investing is not just an option but an imperative. Saving, while essential, is no longer enough to counteract the loss of purchasing power. It is investing that has the power to transform savings into a dynamic source of growth, allowing capital to grow and multiply over time.

In this book, you will be offered the basic principles of investing, such as the importance of diversification, balancing risk and return, and determining an investment horizon. These concepts form the foundation upon which all sophisticated investment strategies are built and are crucial for anyone aspiring to succeed in this field.

With a solid understanding of why investing is vital, the next step is to explore the various strategies you can adopt. There is no universal strategy that works for everyone; what is ideal for one investor may not be for another. That's why this book presents you with a range of approaches, from

"Value Investing," which focuses on finding value in undervalued companies, to "Growth Investing," which seeks to identify companies with explosive growth potential.

Value investing is based on the premise that the market sometimes undervalues the true worth of companies. Identifying these opportunities requires meticulous analysis, and those who master this approach can reap significant rewards when the market eventually recognizes the true value of these companies.

In contrast, Growth Investing focuses on identifying companies that are in a phase of rapid growth and have the potential to generate significantly higher revenues and profits in the future. While this approach may carry higher risks, it also offers the possibility of extraordinary returns for those who choose wisely.

Additionally, the book delves into dividend investing, a strategy that can be particularly attractive to those seeking to generate a steady stream of passive income. Dividend reinvestment is another powerful tool explored here, showing how it can maximize capital growth over time.

Over the decades, investors like Warren Buffett, John Bogle, Ray Dalio, Geraldine Weiss, and many others have perfected their methods, leaving a legacy that remains relevant today. This book invites you to immerse yourself in their investment philosophies, understand their methods, and apply their lessons to your own financial life.

For example, Warren Buffett, known as "The Oracle of Omaha" is a staunch advocate of long-term investing in companies with solid fundamentals. His "buy and hold" strategy has been one of the most successful in investment history.

John Bogle, the pioneer of index funds, revolutionized the investment world with his low-cost, diversified approach. His strategy allows investors to participate in the overall growth of the market without needing to try to outperform it, a task few have consistently achieved.

Ray Dalio, founder of Bridgewater Associates, offers us a unique perspective by combining macroeconomic principles with rigorous discipline and in-depth analysis of global markets. Dalio demonstrates that investing is not just a matter of numbers but also of principles and philosophy.

Thus, this book does not aim to provide definitive answers to all questions about investing. Rather, it is a resource to begin your own learning journey. The world of investing is dynamic and constantly evolving. What works today may not be as effective tomorrow, so it is essential that investors commit to continuous learning and adaptation, knowing that the foundations of investing have worked since time immemorial.

As you progress through this book, you will likely find strategies that resonate with you and others that do not. That is precisely the goal: to provide you with a diverse set of tools and knowledge that you can tailor to your own financial goals and circumstances.

It is important to mention that although this book focuses on some of the most influential investors in history, it has not been possible to include all of them. Investing is a vast field, and many other brilliant investors have also made their mark. We encourage readers to continue exploring and learning from other notable figures whose influence has also been significant.

By starting to read this book, you have taken a crucial step toward building a solid foundation in the world of investing. This book is intended not only as a guide but also as a source of inspiration and a faithful companion on your path to financial success. But remember, the knowledge gained is just the beginning. The true key to success lies in application, experimentation, and perseverance.

The world of investing awaits you. May this bookmark the beginning of a journey full of success and discoveries. Welcome to the exciting and transformative adventure of investing!

Like the great investors

CHAPTER 1:
THE IMPORTANCE OF INVESTING

INTRODUCTION TO INVESTING

WHAT IS INVESTING?

Investing is both an art and a science that has accompanied humanity since the dawn of civilization. From the time when ancient Phoenician merchants traded goods in early markets, through the speculations of the Dutch East India Company, to the modern and complex financial markets of today, the concept of investing has been a constant in the pursuit of wealth and prosperity.

The essence of investing lies in the allocation of resources with the expectation of obtaining a profit or gain in the future. These resources, usually monetary, can be directed toward a wide range of assets or financial instruments. The options are diverse and may include stocks, bonds, real estate, businesses, investment funds, and much more. Each type of investment comes with its own characteristics, risks, and potential benefits, and the choice of where to invest is a crucial decision that must be made with care and planning.

One of the cornerstones of effective investing is careful analysis. Successful investors do not make decisions randomly or rely solely on impulses or passing trends. Instead, they engage in a meticulous process of evaluation and study. This may involve analyzing financial statements, assessing market conditions, studying economic trends, and considering geopolitical factors. All of this is done in order to better understand the asset in which they plan to invest and to anticipate its potential future returns.

Along with careful analysis, a well-defined strategy is essential. Without a clear strategy, investments can become mere bets, and the risk of losses increases significantly. Investors must set clear goals, such as how much money they want to make, the time frame in which they expect to achieve those returns, and the level of risk they are willing to take on. Defining a strategy also involves selecting a diversified portfolio, which can help mitigate the risks associated with investing in a single type of asset.

The time horizon is another crucial factor in investing. Not all investments are suitable for every time horizon. Some investments, such as growth stocks or real estate, may require a longer time frame to mature and yield significant returns. On the other hand, instruments like short-term bonds may be more appropriate for those seeking returns over a shorter period. Understanding one's own time horizon and choosing investments accordingly is vital to achieving financial goals.

Risk tolerance is a personal and individualized aspect that each investor must consider. Not everyone has the same capacity to withstand volatility or the potential losses that may come with investing. Some investors may be willing to take on significant risks in exchange for the possibility of high returns, while others may prefer a more conservative strategy with modest returns but lower risk. Evaluating one's own risk tolerance and aligning the investment strategy with this evaluation is essential to avoid the stress and anxiety associated with market fluctuations.

Finally, diversification is a commonly recommended practice for maximizing the chances of success in investing. By spreading resources across different types of assets and sectors, investors can reduce the negative impact that the poor performance of a single asset might have. Diversification does not guarantee profits or completely protect against losses, but it can help manage risk and smooth out fluctuations in the value of a portfolio over time.

In summary, investing is a complex activity that requires detailed analysis, a clear strategy, an understanding of the time horizon, an assessment of risk tolerance, and proper diversification. It is a combination of art and science, where intuition and information come together to guide investors on their path to obtaining future profits. Investing is not an easy task, but with the right knowledge and preparation, as well as the reading of books like this one, it can be a fruitful path toward achieving financial stability and growth.

A BRIEF HISTORY OF INVESTING

The history of investing is a vast and fascinating journey spanning thousands of years, reflecting humanity's development and continual adaptation in terms of economics, technology, and society.

In the ancient civilizations of Egypt, Mesopotamia, and Rome, investment was firmly rooted in the ownership of land, livestock, and natural resources. This practice not only defined social status and political power, but was also fundamental to economic stability and the long-term generation of wealth.

In Egypt, the pharaohs and nobles accumulated vast tracts of agricultural land, generating income through the production of grains and other crops. The lands of the Nile Valley, fertilized by the river's annual floods, were extremely fertile and productive. The pharaoh, considered a god on earth, was the ultimate owner of all the land, and nobles and high-ranking officials received large portions of land as rewards for their service. These lands were intensively cultivated, mainly producing wheat and barley, essential for feeding the population and for trade. Additionally, controlling these lands allowed the pharaohs and nobles to accumulate vast wealth, which they used to build temples, monuments, and tombs, consolidating their legacy and divine status.

In Mesopotamia, cuneiform records engraved on clay tablets show a complex and well-organized society where investment in land and goods was common practice. The Mesopotamian city-states, such as Uruk, Ur, and Babylon, were surrounded by agricultural lands that were central to their economy. Temples and palaces controlled large tracts of land, worked by peasants and slaves. Land transactions, meticulously recorded, included details about the location, size, and quality of the land, as well as the terms of sale or lease. Besides agriculture, investment in irrigation canals and other hydraulic systems was crucial, as it ensured a constant water supply in a region prone to drought. These infrastructures not only increased agricultural productivity but also prevented conflicts by ensuring the equitable distribution of water among communities.

In Rome, wealth and power were often measured by the amount of land one owned. The patricians, the Roman upper class, controlled vast estates known as latifundia, which were large agricultural plantations worked by slaves. The production of these latifundia, including wheat, olives, and vineyards, not only supplied the city of Rome but also generated income through exports to other regions of the empire. In Rome, land was not only a source of wealth but also of political power. Senators and other high-ranking officials used their properties to influence local and national politics, financing electoral campaigns and gaining the support of their clients and followers. Additionally, Roman army veterans often received land as a reward for their service, providing them with a source of income and helping consolidate Roman control over conquered regions.

Investment in these times focused on stability and the generation of sustainable resources, essential for survival and prosperity. In all these civilizations, the ownership of land and other natural resources was fundamental to the economic and social structure. Agricultural lands provided food and other basic products necessary for daily life, while the control of natural resources, such as water and minerals, ensured the community's well-being and security. Moreover, investment in infrastructure, such as irrigation canals, roads, and warehouses, improved productivity and facilitated trade, fostering economic growth and social cohesion.

With the advent of the Middle Ages, the landscape of investing began to change significantly. This era saw the rise of the first forms of international trade and banking, phenomena that would be crucial for the economic development of Europe and the world in the centuries to come. Medieval merchants and bankers played a key role in financing commercial expeditions and productive activities, opening new routes and markets.

Italian merchants, for example, developed highly sophisticated credit and bill of exchange systems for their time. These financial innovations made it possible to finance long trading journeys, facilitating the movement of goods and money across vast distances. Bills of exchange were documents that authorized the payment of a sum of money at a future date, providing a safe and efficient way to transfer funds without the need to transport large quantities of gold or silver. This system not only reduced the risk of loss or theft but also sped up transactions and fostered trust between merchants.

The city-states of Venice and Genoa became nerve centers of commerce and banking in Europe. Thanks to their strategic location and powerful maritime fleets, these cities dominated trade in the Mediterranean and beyond. Venetian and Genoese merchants took on significant risks by financing commercial expeditions that could last months or even years. These expeditions, often to the Far East, brought back exotic goods like spices, silk, and gems, which were highly valuable in European markets.

In Venice, the city's political and social structure fostered the growth of trade and banking. The Republic of Venice, governed by an oligarchy of merchants and nobles, established a legal and administrative system that supported and regulated commercial activities. Venetians developed detailed maritime contracts known as "collegantia" which specified the terms and conditions of trade expeditions, including the distribution of profits and risks between investors and ship captains. This system allowed for greater risk diversification and encouraged investment in multiple expeditions.

Genoa, on the other hand, was renowned for its innovations in banking and credit. Genoese bankers were known for their ability to manage large sums of money and their capacity to finance large-scale projects. The Bank of Saint George, founded in the 15th century, was one of the first in Europe to offer deposit and lending services, playing a crucial role in financing Genoese commercial ventures. Genoese bankers also developed early forms of bonds and other financial instruments, allowing investors to diversify their portfolios and minimize risk.

Investment during this era was no longer limited solely to land but began to encompass trade and production. The trade routes connecting Europe with Asia and Africa brought a steady flow of goods and wealth, stimulating the growth of cities and the development of new technologies and production methods. Guilds, associations of artisans and merchants, played an important role in regulating production and trade, establishing quality standards and prices, and providing mutual support to their members. These guilds also facilitated training and apprenticeships, ensuring a steady supply of skilled workers.

Additionally, investment in infrastructure such as ports, warehouses, and trade routes were fundamental to economic growth. Port cities like Venice and Genoa invested in the construction of docks and shipyards, improving their capacity to handle large volumes of trade and maintain their maritime fleets. Overland trade routes, such as the Camino de Santiago, were also developed and improved, facilitating the movement of people and goods across Europe.

The Renaissance and the Age of Discovery marked a crucial turning point in the history of investment, laying the foundations for the modern economy. This period, spanning the 15th to 17th centuries, witnessed the growth of international trade and major explorations that drove investment in commercial enterprises in unprecedented ways.

The growth of international trade was one of the main drivers of this transformation. European cities became prosperous trading hubs, and merchants began to seek new routes and markets beyond the traditional boundaries of Europe. The search for spices, gold, silk, and other valuable products led Europeans to undertake long expeditions to Asia, Africa, and the Americas. These journeys were extremely costly and dangerous, requiring significant financing. Investors, attracted by the possibility of great profits, began funding these expeditions.

The East India companies became the most prominent commercial entities of the time, symbolizing the new approach to investment and trade.

The Dutch East India Company, founded in 1602, is a prime example. The Dutch East India Company was the first to issue shares and bonds to finance its operations, establishing one of the world's first stock markets. Investors bought shares in the company, expecting to receive dividends from the profits generated by the trade of spices, silk, and other exotic goods brought from Asia.

The organizational structure of the Dutch East India Company and its innovative financial approach marked a milestone in the history of investment. The company not only raised funds through the sale of shares, but also issued bonds to finance its expeditions and commercial operations. This practice allowed the Dutch East India Company to gather large sums of capital, which it used to build and equip a fleet of ships, establish trading posts and fortifications in Asia, and hire a large workforce of employees and soldiers. The issuance of shares and bonds also facilitated the diversification of risk among a large number of investors, making investments safer and more attractive.

The success of the Dutch East India Company inspired the formation of similar companies in other countries. The British East India Company, founded in 1600 and contemporary with the Dutch East India Company, followed a similar model, using the sale of shares to finance its operations in India and other parts of Asia. These companies played a crucial role in the expansion of international trade and the establishment of colonial empires, and their financial innovations laid the groundwork for the development of modern stock markets.

This era also saw the development of other financial instruments and investment methods. Banking underwent a significant transformation during this period, with the emergence of banks offering a wider range of financial services. Italian bankers, particularly in Florence and Venice, developed advanced accounting and financing methods that allowed merchants to better manage their investments and reduce the risks associated with long-distance trade. Bills of exchange, which had already been used during the Middle Ages, became more common and sophisticated, facilitating trade financing and the transfer of money across borders.

Furthermore, the development of maritime insurance helped mitigate the risks associated with commercial expeditions. Insurance policies covered potential losses due to shipwrecks, piracy, and other dangers, allowing merchants and investors to take greater risks with increased security. These financial innovations fostered a safer and more attractive environment for investment, encouraging more people to participate in trade and finance new ventures.

Moving forward, the Industrial Revolution of the 18th century radically transformed the investment landscape, marking the beginning of an era of unprecedented economic growth. With the advent of new technologies and production methods, investment in machinery, factories, and railroads became a common and essential practice for industrial development.

Technological innovations of the time, such as James Watt's steam engine and Edmund Cartwright's mechanical loom, revolutionized manufacturing production. These machines allowed for more efficient mass production at lower costs, significantly increasing the demand for capital to build and equip factories. Entrepreneurs needed to invest in advanced machinery and the construction of large industrial facilities to take advantage of the new technologies. This need for financing led to the development of new methods to mobilize capital.

The emergence of modern capital markets was one of the most significant responses to this need. The first stock exchanges in London and New York were established during this period, providing an organized space where investors could buy and sell shares of companies. The London Stock Exchange, founded in 1801, and the New York Stock Exchange, founded in 1792, allowed for the mobilization of large amounts of capital to finance industrial projects. These stock exchanges became nerve centers of investment, where stocks and bonds were traded to finance the expansion of industry and infrastructure.

Investment during this period was driven by growth and innovation. Investors saw new technologies and industrial production methods as an opportunity for great profits. Shares of manufacturing and railway companies became highly sought-after assets, offering the potential for high returns as the companies grew and prospered. The construction of railroads, in particular, attracted enormous amounts of capital. Railroads not only facilitated the transport of goods and people but also stimulated regional economic development by connecting markets and reducing transportation costs.

In addition to investments in machinery and railroads, the Industrial Revolution also saw an increase in investment in urban infrastructure. Cities were growing rapidly due to urbanization and rural migration, requiring improvements in public services such as water, sanitation, and transportation. Entrepreneurs and local governments invested in the construction of aqueducts, sewage systems, and paved streets to improve living conditions in cities and support industrial growth.

The economic dynamism of the Industrial Revolution also brought about a series of social transformations. The creation of factory jobs and the development of new labor opportunities in cities attracted large numbers of people from rural areas to urban centers. This demographic shift boosted the demand for goods and services, which in turn fueled economic growth. However, challenges also arose, such as harsh working conditions in factories and the need for labor regulations to protect workers.

By the 20th century, transformation occurred thanks to the unprecedented expansion of financial markets and the creation of new investment instruments, profoundly and permanently reshaping the global economic landscape. This period was characterized by financial innovation and the globalization of markets, allowing investors to better manage risk and maximize returns.

One of the most significant developments of the 20th century was the creation and popularization of mutual funds. These instruments allowed individual investors to access diversified portfolios of stocks and bonds managed by professionals. Mutual funds reduced the risk associated with investing in individual assets, offering investors the opportunity to participate in a broader market without the need for large sums of capital.

In addition to mutual funds, the 20th century saw the creation and development of financial derivatives. Derivatives, such as options and futures, offered new ways to manage risk and speculate on price movements. These instruments allowed investors to protect themselves against adverse fluctuations in the prices of underlying assets, ensuring greater financial stability. Derivatives also facilitated the emergence of more complex and dynamic markets, contributing to the efficiency and liquidity of global financial markets. However, these instruments also attracted speculators seeking to make large profits in a short period. This short-term and high-risk mindset led to significant losses for individual investors, who saw investment more as an exciting gamble than a means to preserve and grow wealth.

Modern portfolio theory, developed by Harry Markowitz in the 1950s, provided a theoretical framework for diversification and risk management. Markowitz introduced the concept that a well-diversified portfolio can maximize expected returns for a given level of risk or minimize risk for a given level of expected return. His work laid the foundation for modern investment management, emphasizing the importance of considering covariance (a value that indicates the degree of joint variation between two random variables relative to their means) between assets when constructing a diversified portfolio. This theory transformed how investors and fund managers thought about diversification and portfolio optimization.

Fundamental analysis, popularized by Benjamin Graham and David Dodd in their influential book "Security Analysis" published in 1934, provided tools to evaluate the intrinsic value of stocks. This approach focused on the detailed analysis of a company's financial statements, including its revenues, expenses, assets, and liabilities, to determine its real value. Graham and Dodd argued that by identifying discrepancies between a stock's intrinsic value and its market price, investors could make more informed and profitable investment decisions. Fundamental analysis became a widely adopted method for stock selection, forming the basis of value investing.

The 20th century also saw the globalization of financial markets, with investors from around the world participating in capital markets. Advances in communication and technology, such as the telegraph, telephone, and later the internet, facilitated the interconnection of global financial markets. Investors could now access different markets in various parts of the world, further diversifying their portfolios and taking advantage of investment opportunities on a global scale. This globalization also led to greater economic and financial integration among countries, increasing the interdependence of world economies.

The creation of international organizations, such as the International Monetary Fund (IMF) and the World Bank, also played a crucial role in financial globalization. These institutions provided financial and technical support to countries, promoting global economic and financial stability. Additionally, the liberalization of capital markets in many parts of the world allowed for greater capital mobility, fostering foreign direct investment and economic growth.

As we entered the 21st century, we must talk about technologies that have revolutionized investment in unimaginable ways, profoundly transforming how individuals and institutions manage their finances. Technological innovations have democratized access to financial markets like never before, making investing more accessible, efficient, and personalized.

One of the most significant advancements has been the rise of online trading platforms. These platforms have allowed individuals from all over the world to easily buy and sell stocks, bonds, and other financial instruments. Previously, investing in financial markets was primarily reserved for professionals and those with access to stockbrokers. However, with online trading platforms, anyone with internet access can participate in financial markets. These platforms offer advanced tools, real-time data, and reduced commissions, leveling the playing field and making investment more inclusive than ever.

Artificial intelligence (AI) and data analysis have further revolutionized investing in the 21st century. Advanced technologies enable the analysis of large volumes of data at high speeds and with unprecedented precision. AI algorithms can identify patterns and trends in financial markets, developing more sophisticated and personalized investment strategies. These algorithms can not only analyze historical data but also learn and adapt to new information, continually improving their predictions and decisions. AI is used in a variety of applications, from fraud detection to portfolio optimization, transforming how investors manage risk and seek returns.

Blockchain technology and cryptocurrencies have also emerged as disruptive innovations in the 21st century. Blockchain, the technology underlying cryptocurrencies like Bitcoin and Ethereum, offers a secure and transparent way to record transactions. This technology has the potential to transform not only how financial transactions are conducted but also a wide range of industries, from supply chains to voting systems. Cryptocurrencies have created new investment opportunities, though they have also introduced new challenges and risks due to their high volatility and lack of regulation.

The history of investment is a testament to human ingenuity and adaptability, showing how investment practices have evolved and adapted over the centuries to respond to changing economic, technological, and social conditions. From the fertile lands of the Nile to the algorithms of Wall Street, investment has been a crucial tool for wealth creation and economic progress, reflecting our ability to innovate and find new ways to manage capital.

DIFFERENCES BETWEEN SAVING AND INVESTING

Although often used interchangeably in everyday conversations, the concepts of saving and investing are fundamental in personal and business financial management, and they are clearly distinguished by their characteristics, objectives, and consequences. Understanding these differences is crucial for making informed financial decisions that align with individual needs and goals.

Saving is a fundamental financial practice that involves setting aside a portion of income for future use. This money is kept in safe, easily accessible places, such as bank accounts, where it remains liquid and retains its nominal value. The primary purpose of saving is to provide security and easy access to capital, allowing people to have funds available when needed to cover unexpected expenses, finance short-term major purchases, or maintain an emergency fund.

One of the most notable features of saving is its low level of risk. Savings accounts are typically insured by government entities, ensuring that even if the financial institution encounters problems, the savings are protected up to a certain limit. For example, in many countries, savings accounts are insured by organizations like the Federal Deposit Insurance Corporation (FDIC) in the United States or the Deposit Guarantee Fund for Credit Institutions (FGD) in Spain. This protection gives savers peace of mind, knowing that their money is safe even in times of economic uncertainty. This security is one of the reasons many people choose to keep a portion of their money in savings accounts, especially those who prefer to avoid any financial risk.

In addition to security, accessibility is another important advantage of saving. Savings accounts allow account holders to withdraw funds easily, whether through ATMs, electronic transfers, or visits to the bank branch. This accessibility is crucial in emergency situations where cash is needed quickly. Having savings can mean the difference between covering an unexpected expense, like an urgent car repair or an unforeseen medical bill, and having to resort to costly debt.

However, the return on savings is typically low. The interest rates offered by financial institutions on savings accounts are usually modest and, in many cases, do not exceed the inflation rate. Inflation, which is the generalized increase in the prices of goods and services over time, can erode the purchasing power of saved money. This means that, although saved money is safe, its ability to buy goods and services may decrease over time due to inflation. For example, if the interest rate on a savings account is 1% annually, but the inflation rate is 2%, the purchasing power of the money in the account will decrease in real terms by at least 1%. This means, and to the surprise of many, that keeping money in a low or non-interest-bearing account can, with certainty, make us poorer over time.

Despite its low return, saving remains an essential tool for short-term financial management and maintaining financial stability. For many, saving represents a first line of defense against financial difficulties. It is also an effective way to plan for short-term financial goals, such as a trip, a wedding, or the purchase of an appliance. Additionally, having a savings cushion can provide a sense of security and reduce financial stress, knowing that resources are available to face unforeseen events.

Saving can also be the first step toward building broader financial wealth. Many people begin their financial journey by establishing a savings base before exploring investment options that may offer higher returns. By keeping a portion of their income in a safe and accessible savings account, individuals can accumulate the capital needed to make more ambitious investments in the future, such as buying a home, starting a business, or investing in the stock market.

As we have seen, saving is fundamental as a first step toward building financial wealth. However, we must be aware that saving alone will not work miracles, and it is necessary to adopt a more active approach if we want this wealth to grow over time. To do this, it is necessary to invest part of the capital we have managed to save.

Investing involves allocating resources, usually money, to assets that have the potential to appreciate or generate income over time. Unlike saving, where the primary goal is the security and accessibility of capital, investing aims to generate a significant return that can exceed inflation and increase the investor's purchasing power. Investments can be made in a variety of assets, including stocks, bonds, real estate, businesses, mutual funds, and more.

One of the main objectives of investing is to outperform inflation. Inflation erodes the purchasing power of money over time, so investing in assets that can grow in value is essential to maintaining and increasing purchasing power. For example, if the annual inflation rate is 2%, an investment that generates a 5% annual return not only maintains the value of the money but also increases it, providing a real gain of 3%.

Investments carry a considerably higher level of risk than saving. The values of investments can fluctuate due to a variety of factors, including market conditions, economic changes, and company-specific events. This volatility is an inherent characteristic of financial markets. For example, the price of a stock can rise or fall quickly in response to a company's quarterly earnings reports, changes in government policy, or geopolitical events, or even market sentiment or external news unrelated to the company itself. However, this risk also carries the possibility of higher returns. Successful investments can provide significant gains, making investing a powerful tool for wealth creation and achieving long-term financial goals.

Investment returns can vary widely. While some investments may generate high returns, others may not perform as well or may even result in losses. For example, investing in a startup can yield exceptional returns if the company succeeds, but there is also the possibility that the company will fail and the investment will be lost. This variability in returns is a crucial consideration for investors, who must assess their risk tolerance and time horizon before making investment decisions.

An investor's risk tolerance determines the amount of risk they are willing to take on. Some investors prefer low-risk investments, such as government bonds, which offer more stable but lower returns. Others may opt for high-risk investments, such as stocks of emerging tech companies, which can offer potentially high returns but come with a greater possibility of loss. The time horizon, or the period during which an investor plans to hold an investment, is also an important factor. Investors with a long-term horizon may be willing to take on more risk, as they have more time to recover from potential losses.

Despite the risks, investing is essential for those looking to grow their capital and achieve more ambitious financial goals. Investments can help finance major long-term objectives, such as retirement, children's education, or buying a home. For example, investing in a retirement fund can provide the necessary resources for a comfortable retirement, while investing in a diversified portfolio of stocks and bonds can generate the capital growth needed to pay for children's college education.

Additionally, investing can play a crucial role in economic growth. Investments in innovative companies and projects can drive technological development, create jobs, and improve productivity. Investors who provide capital to new businesses are supporting innovation and entrepreneurship, which in turn can generate broader economic benefits.

Key differences:

    - Purpose: Saving is intended to preserve capital and maintain liquidity, providing security and accessibility. Investing seeks to generate significant long-term returns, using capital to create wealth.

    - Risk: Savings are exposed to very low risk, with protection guaranteed by government entities. Investments carry higher risk due to market volatility and other economic factors, but also offer the possibility of greater returns.

- Return: The return on savings is low and, in most cases, does not exceed inflation, which can lead to a reduction in purchasing power over time. The return on investments can be significantly higher, but is also subject to variability and risk.

WHY INVESTING IS CRUCIAL

THE IMPACT OF INFLATION ON PURCHASING POWER

Inflation is a complex economic phenomenon that, while it may seem like an abstract concept, has tangible and significant effects on people's daily lives. Inflation refers to the widespread and sustained increase in the prices of goods and services in an economy over a period of time. This price increase directly impacts purchasing power, or the ability of money to buy goods and services, and its effects are deeply felt across all aspects of economic and financial life.

- Loss of Money's Value: To illustrate how inflation affects purchasing power, consider a scenario where the inflation rate is 3% annually. In this context, an item that costs $100 today will cost $103 in a year. While the difference of $3 may seem insignificant in the short term, the compounded effect of inflation becomes much more significant over time. After ten years, that same item will cost approximately $134. If a person has saved $100 without investing it, the real value of their money will have eroded drastically; their savings will still be $100, but now it will only buy what used to cost $74, losing about 25% of its initial purchasing power.

This phenomenon extends to all goods and services, from everyday consumer products to major investments like housing and education. The loss of money's value means that people need more money to maintain the same standard of living, which can lead to a reduction in savings and increased financial pressure on households.

- Erosion of Savings: The erosion of purchasing power also significantly impacts savings. People who save money in traditional savings accounts, which generally offer very low interest rates, often find that their savings do not grow enough to counter inflation. As discussed in relation to saving, if the interest rate on a savings account is 1% annually and the inflation rate is 3%, the savings are actually losing value in real terms at a rate of 2% per year.

This reality highlights the importance of finding investment strategies that can offer returns higher than the inflation rate. Otherwise, even prudently saved money may not be enough to meet long-term financial goals, such as retirement, children's education, or buying a home.

- Need for Investments That Outperform Inflation: To mitigate the effects of inflation and protect purchasing power, it is essential that savings be invested in assets that offer returns above the inflation rate. There are several investment options that have historically provided returns greater than inflation, including stocks, real estate, and certain types of bonds.

Stocks, for example, represent ownership in a company and have proven to be one of the most effective ways to generate wealth in the long term. Although stocks can be volatile in the short term, over the long term, they tend to outperform inflation, providing real growth in capital. Similarly, real estate offers protection against inflation, as property prices and rental income tend to rise with inflation.

Bonds, particularly inflation-linked bonds like TIPS (Treasury Inflation-Protected Securities) in the United States, can also be a useful tool. These bonds adjust their principal value and interest payments according to inflation, offering a safer investment option for those seeking protection against the erosion of purchasing power.

- Financial Planning and Education: Understanding inflation and its impact on purchasing power is fundamental to effective financial planning. People need to be aware of how inflation can affect their savings and actively seek investment opportunities that can provide real capital growth. Financial education plays a crucial role in this, helping individuals make informed decisions about where and how to invest their money to achieve their financial goals.

Additionally, investment diversification is a key strategy for managing risk and ensuring that returns not only preserve but increase purchasing power. Diversifying means investing in a variety of assets that respond differently to market conditions, helping to balance risk and rewards.

Compound interest is one of the most powerful forces in finance, often referred to as "the eighth wonder of the world." It is a simple concept at its core, but has profound and far-reaching implications for the growth of invested money. Compound interest not only builds on the initial capital invested but also on the accumulated interest from previous periods. This characteristic allows funds to grow exponentially over time, transforming small sums into considerable fortunes when given enough time to mature.

THE MAGIC OF COMPOUND INTEREST

It is believed that Albert Einstein once said, "Compound interest is the eighth wonder of the world. He who understands it, earns it. He who doesn't, pays it." This point is so important that I believe anyone who truly understands it will never be the same person again, so let's dive in.

Unlike simple interest, which is calculated only on the initial principal, compound interest takes into account the interest generated in previous periods and adds it to the principal for future interest calculations. This process creates a multiplier effect, where the invested money grows at an exponential rate. For example, if you invest $1,000 at a 5% annual simple interest rate, after 10 years, the total amount would be $1,500. This is because each year you receive $50 on your $1,000 investment. However, with annual compound interest, the total amount after 10 years would be approximately $1,629. This effect becomes even more pronounced over time: after 20 years, the total would be $2,000 with simple interest, but with compound interest, it would reach approximately $2,653.

This exponential growth of capital is at the heart of compound interest. Each year, not only the initial principal but also the accumulated interest generates new interest. This dynamic creates a cycle of continuous and accelerated growth, making compound interest a powerful tool for wealth accumulation. It highlights that the longer the money is invested, the greater the potential gains. Hence, it's crucial to start investing as early as possible with the capital saved, as the rewards will be larger over time. To further emphasize the importance of time in compound interest, let's explore an example with a more stressed scenario to make the previous point clearer.

Suppose a person invests $10,000 at an annual interest rate of 5%. After 10 years, this person would have a total of $16,289. If this person decides to keep the investment for another 20 years, they would accumulate $43,219. Now, imagine that this individual still doesn't need the money and decides to reserve it for retirement, so they leave it invested for an additional 20 years at the same 5% annual interest rate. After a total of 50 years, this person would have $114,674. As we can see, the scenario changes dramatically when the investment is extended over time, and the benefits are not withdrawn. This is why Einstein considered compound interest the eighth wonder of the world, as long-term results tend to be astonishing.

But the wonder of compound interest doesn't stop here. So far, we've been working with a 5% annual interest rate, a figure that, at first glance, seems easily achievable. Now, imagine that you're someone with higher ambitions, and after some education and years of experience, you start earning an 8% annual interest rate, which is still a relatively attainable rate. If we use the same figures from the previous example, we will see how the scenario changes radically again. After 10 years of investing $10,000 at an 8% annual interest rate, the total amount would be $21,589. After 30 years, it would be $100,626. And after 50 years, it would reach $469,026. As we can see, the amounts start to become significantly larger. With these examples, it is clear why compound interest is considered the eighth wonder of the world, and it's essential to understand that time works in our favor.

To maximize the benefits of compound interest, it's essential to implement investment strategies that fully leverage its potential. One of the most effective strategies is dividend reinvestment. Many mutual funds and stocks pay regular dividends. By reinvesting these dividends instead of withdrawing them, investors can harness the power of compound interest to further grow their capital.

Another key strategy is consistency in contributions. Even small, regular contributions can accumulate significantly over time thanks to compound interest. This is particularly important for retirement accounts and long-term savings funds.

Additionally, maintaining a long-term perspective and resisting the temptation to withdraw funds prematurely is crucial. Discipline and patience are essential to allow compound interest to work at its full potential. Imagining that this is money you won't touch for a long time, or even ignoring its existence, can make it easier to keep the capital invested and take full advantage of compound interest.

ACHIEVING FINANCIAL INDEPENDENCE

This book is not written with the purpose of having readers blindly pursue financial independence, but rather to make them aware of the importance of investing for maintaining good economic health and acquiring the basic knowledge needed to start investing. While there is no doubt that financial independence is on the horizon for every investor who embarks on the long and arduous path of investing, it is crucial to clarify that financial independence is not an easy goal and is not suitable for everyone. The journey toward financial independence involves many variables that will affect us, and only a few will ultimately achieve it.

Once this objective fact is understood, do not be discouraged. In the world of investing, it's about finding a balance. As we have discussed, the investment journey is long and arduous, and over time, it will become an intrinsic part of each person's way of being. However, one must never forget that we live only once, and it's necessary to balance the enjoyment of the present life with the savings we keep invested for the enjoyment of our future life. This balance becomes crucial when we understand that financial health is not about a financial diet but rather a paradigm shift and a turning point in life, where we begin to realize that living does not require a certain level of consumption, and that money becomes a tool for achieving a certain degree of freedom, rather than being exclusively for the consumption of goods and services.

What is financial independence?

Financial independence is a dream for many: the freedom to live without the constraints of active employment or reliance on a regular salary. This independence is achieved when a person has sufficient passive income, savings, or investments to cover their living expenses consistently. Reaching this goal requires careful planning, financial discipline, and a deep understanding of the crucial role that investing plays in long-term wealth creation.

One of the fundamental pillars for achieving financial independence is generating passive income. Unlike active income, which requires continuous effort (such as a salary), passive income is generated with little or no ongoing involvement. There are several ways to generate this income, each with its own advantages and challenges.

Investing in real estate is one of the most popular ways to generate passive income. Buying rental properties not only provides monthly income but can also offer long-term capital appreciation. Managing properties may require some effort, but with good management or by hiring a property management company, owners can enjoy a steady flow of income.

On the other hand, investing in dividend-paying stocks is another effective strategy. Successful companies often distribute a portion of their profits to shareholders in the form of dividends. These payments can be reinvested to benefit from compound interest or used to cover expenses, providing a stable source of passive income.

Another option is through bonds and other financial instruments. Bonds are loans that investors make to government or corporate entities in exchange for regular interest payments. Investing in bonds can offer a fixed income, although generally with lower returns compared to stocks.

Other instruments such as mutual funds and certificates of deposit can also contribute to generating passive income.

Consider the case of Ana, a young woman who begins investing $500 monthly at age 25 in a diversified portfolio with an average annual return of 7%. Ana understands the importance of consistency and discipline, and continues to invest this amount religiously each month.

By age 35, after a decade of consistent investments, Ana has accumulated approximately $83,754. The magic of compound interest starts to become evident, and the capital begins to grow more rapidly.

By the time Ana turns 45, her portfolio has grown to around $237,701. The combination of her regular contributions and compound interest continues to work in her favor, accelerating capital growth. At this point, Ana feels that this amount is sufficient to cover her living expenses, and instead of continuing to grow her capital, she decides that the 7% annual return is adequate. So, Ana starts withdrawing 7% of her capital annually, which amounts to about $1,380 per month to cover her expenses, while keeping the $237,701 intact.

Although this could be a possible strategy, there is a clear flaw for those who view it as a perfect strategy. Both the $237,701 and the $1,380 monthly withdrawals, thanks to the interest, are currently sufficient, but they are likely to fall short in 10 years. This is due to the effect of inflation, which we have discussed several times in these initial pages. This clearly demonstrates how inflation is a significant variable that can derail our financial plans.

If Ana decides to live off the passive income generated, she could not withdraw 7% of her capital but should subtract the inflation rate from the interest earned on her invested money. In our example, if inflation were at 3% annually, Ana could only withdraw 4% of the capital to achieve a capital appreciation of at least 3% corresponding to inflation, thus maintaining her future purchasing power.

The best strategy for Ana would be to continue accumulating capital and depend on her active income for a longer period, with the goal of building enough capital to avoid future problems. If Ana had waited until age 65, that is, 40 years of consistent investing, she would have accumulated about $1,200,000, which again provides a clear example of the power of compound interest over the years, and especially, how much more significant the investment becomes the longer it is maintained.

Therefore, we must understand that financial independence is a journey that begins with saving and subsequently investing that savings. Additionally, we need to be consistent in contributions to accumulate enough capital to generate passive income. After sufficient time has passed, we should analyze our situation, such as the level of living expenses to be covered by passive income, the need to stop working, and other variables to decide the optimal time or sufficient capital to start our financial independence.

We must clarify that psychology plays a crucial role in the world of investing. In presenting the previous example, we have likely oversimplified the investment world. No investment is linear, and many variables can affect both the investor and the investment. Crises, bankruptcies, poor capital allocation, etc.—all these situations can lead to moments when our capital might be reduced by a significant percentage. For instance, rather than consistently earning a 7% annual return, it is more realistic to experience irregular returns over the years, such as 15% in the first year, 20% in the second year, -30% in the third year, 0% in the fourth year, and so on. This non-linearity can cause investors to become discouraged after a bad year or, in the worst-case scenario, succumb to the fear of losing their capital and decide to withdraw their investment, potentially leaving the investment world at the worst possible moment and feeling that investing is a scam designed to trap the unwary.

Therefore, patience and good financial psychology are essential to navigating the complex moments that everyone must face at some point on the long and arduous journey of investing.

BASIC INVESTMENT PRINCIPLES

DIVERSIFICATION

Diversification is a fundamental investment strategy that involves spreading financial resources across different types of assets and sectors to reduce risk. This principle is based on the idea of not putting "all your eggs in one basket." Diversifying a portfolio helps protect against market volatility and significant losses in case an asset or sector underperforms.

One of the main objectives of diversification is to mitigate the specific risk associated with a single investment. This type of risk, also known as unsystematic risk, affects a particular company or sector. For example, if an investor holds shares only in a technology company and that company encounters significant problems, the value of the investment can drop drastically, and in the worst case, disappear entirely. However, if the investor diversifies their investments across multiple companies in different sectors, a decline in the value of one investment can be offset by the positive performance of others.

Furthermore, diversifying across different sectors and geographies helps balance the portfolio, as different sectors may react differently to economic conditions. For instance, during a recession, certain sectors like technology may be more affected than defensive sectors such as food and healthcare. By having a mix of investments in uncorrelated sectors, greater stability in the overall portfolio performance can be achieved.

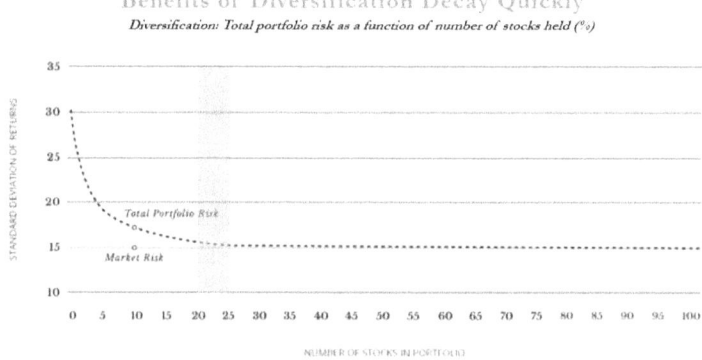

This table is based on a study discussed in the book A Random Walk Down Wall Street, written by Burton Malkiel in 1973. Malkiel's graph illustrates that by adding more stocks to a portfolio, volatility decreases, demonstrating the principle of diversification. However, Malkiel notes that even a portfolio with all the stocks in the world cannot eliminate volatility completely; it can only be reduced to the general market volatility level (labeled as "market risk" in the table). It is evident that a portfolio of individual stocks will be much more volatile than the market as a whole.

If your goal as an investor is to match the market's performance, then broad diversification is essential. But what if you want to outperform the market? The only way to do that is to have a portfolio that differs from the market. The graph shows that having approximately 20-25 stocks in a portfolio is sufficient to capture nearly all the benefits of diversification.

A key premise of this graph is that stocks are selected randomly. If you acquire 20-25 stocks from the same sector, such as oil or banking, your portfolio will remain more volatile than the market due to the high correlation among these stocks. Companies within the same sector tend to move together, preventing their volatilities from offsetting each other. However, an active investor aiming to outperform the market can approach this ideal by selecting stocks from different sectors, ensuring they are not too correlated and belong to various markets and business models.

For an active investor, adding too many companies to a portfolio can be costly and counterproductive. As Phil Fisher says, including too many names leads to investing "too little in well-known companies and too much in others about which little is known."

Searching for stocks that outperform the market is a considerable challenge. The biggest hurdle is finding enough stocks that significantly outperform the market. This is a continuous process, as a stock that performs better than the market is less likely to maintain that performance in the future, requiring the investor to find new opportunities. Therefore, for active investors, there is a significant cost in adding new names to a portfolio.

According to Malkiel's table, the optimal point for an active investor seeking to outperform the market is 20 to 25 companies, although there are other theories suggesting that 8 to 12 well-selected companies might be sufficient to mitigate most of the risk.

Types of Diversification:

- Asset Diversification: This strategy involves distributing financial resources across different types of assets and sectors to reduce risk. This principle is based on the idea of not putting "all your eggs in one basket." Diversifying a portfolio helps protect against market volatility and significant losses if a single asset or sector performs poorly. Stocks can offer high returns but also carry higher risk, while bonds are generally safer but provide lower returns. Real estate can provide stable income and long-term capital appreciation, and cash offers liquidity and security. By combining these different types of assets, an investor can balance the risk and return of their portfolio.

Some investors disagree with this type of diversification, believing that the returns from stocks are much higher compared to other assets, and thus see investing in other assets as an opportunity cost. Warren Buffett, for example, typically focuses on stocks and, to a lesser extent, on liquidity and bonds, investing primarily when stock valuations are perceived as reasonable. On the other hand, investors like Ray Dalio maintain greater asset diversification through his "All Weather Portfolio," allocating 40% of his capital to long-term bonds, 30% to stocks, 15% to short-term fixed income, 7.5% to commodities, and 7.5% to gold.

- Geographic Diversification: This involves investing in international markets to take advantage of global growth opportunities and reduce dependence on the economy of a single country. Different regions and countries may have different economic cycles, and by diversifying geographically, an investor can protect against economic and political fluctuations that might affect a specific country. For example, a recession in one country may be offset by economic growth in another.

It is important to note that when investing in different countries or regions, one must be aware of the local currencies in which they are investing. For instance, if investing in the UK but residing in Europe, you will be dealing with British pounds, while your reference currency is the Euro. This might seem trivial at first but can cause significant variations in returns due to currency fluctuations. Thus, attention must be paid to currency risks when making diversified investments.

- Sector Diversification: This involves investing in different sectors of the economy, such as technology, healthcare, finance, and energy, to reduce the impact of sector-specific volatility. Each economic sector has its own cycles and can be affected by specific factors. By diversifying across sectors, an investor can protect against volatility that may affect a particular sector. For example, if the energy sector is affected by a drop in oil prices, other sectors like technology or healthcare might not be as impacted, or even sectors like aviation could benefit significantly.

It is important to understand that this diversification often depends on the economic cycle we are in. The global economy moves through a series of recurring phases known as economic cycles. These cycles consist of periods of expansion and contraction that significantly impact investment opportunities. Understanding these cycles and adjusting investment strategies according to the phases is crucial for maximizing returns and minimizing risks. Howard Marks, an expert in this type of investing, provides valuable insights in his book "The Most Important Thing: Uncommon

Sense for the Thoughtful Investor." Here is a brief summary of the general characteristics of each economic cycle phase to help identify each phase and recommend possible investments.

The expansion phase is characterized by sustained economic growth, an increase in industrial production, low unemployment rates, and rising consumer confidence. During this phase, GDP increases, and businesses experience higher revenues and profits. It is generally advisable to invest in cyclical sectors that tend to perform well when the economy is booming, such as technology companies, consumer discretionary sectors—businesses that produce non-essential goods and services—as well as industrial and manufacturing sectors.

At the peak of the economic cycle, where growth reaches its maximum before beginning to slow down, a shift in strategy is necessary. Inflation may rise, and interest rates often increase as a measure to cool down an overheating economy. During this phase, it is prudent to begin shifting investments toward more defensive sectors that tend to be less affected by an economic slowdown, such as healthcare companies, consumer staples (companies that produce essential goods), and utility companies (electricity, water, gas), which are generally less impacted by economic fluctuations.

During the contraction phase, characterized by a slowdown in economic growth, rising unemployment, decreased production, and low consumer confidence—which can lead to a recession if the contraction is severe and prolonged—it is crucial to invest in sectors that offer stability and recession resilience. In this phase, we can maintain our investments in healthcare and consumer staples companies, while alternatively, part of the capital can be diverted to assets like Treasury bonds, as well as gold and precious metals, which tend to hold or even appreciate in value during times of economic uncertainty.

Lastly, we have the recovery phase, which begins when the economy starts to emerge from a recession. During this phase, there is an improvement in production, a decrease in unemployment, and a gradual restoration of consumer confidence. During recovery, it is strategic to start positioning in sectors that benefit from the start of a new expansion cycle, such as cyclical stocks, particularly technology and consumer discretionary sectors, which tend to show signs of recovery before others. Additionally, part of our capital can be allocated to infrastructure investments, as there is often an increase in infrastructure projects to stimulate economic growth. Finally, during this phase, it is advisable to invest in small and medium-sized enterprises, as they often recover and grow faster than large corporations at the beginning of an economic expansion.

Temporal Diversification: This involves investing at different times rather than all at once. The investment strategy known as "dollar-cost averaging" involves investing a fixed amount of money at regular intervals, regardless of the asset's price. This can reduce the risk of investing a large sum of money just before a significant market decline. It also helps in understanding investment as a habit reinforced by each contribution made. Over time, these contributions can accumulate substantial capital, insulated from short-term market fluctuations.

- Diversification by Investment Styles: This involves using different investment styles, such as value and growth. Value stocks are those undervalued relative to their financial fundamentals, while growth stocks are companies expected to grow at a faster rate than the market average. Having a mix of both styles can provide a balance between growth potential and stability.

- Diversification in Investment Funds and ETFs: For individual investors, mutual funds and exchange-traded funds (ETFs) offer an easy way to diversify. These funds pool money from many investors to buy a wide range of assets, providing instant diversification. ETFs, in particular, can offer diversification in specific sectors, geographies, or investment styles and can be traded like stocks on an exchange.

If you haven't fully grasped the concepts of diversification in the last two points, don't worry; this book will explore investment styles and various financial instruments, including mutual funds and ETFs, in more depth.

Diversifying a portfolio can involve additional costs, such as transaction fees and fund management fees. It is important to consider these costs when designing a diversification strategy to ensure they do not erode potential benefits. Additionally, a diversified portfolio requires regular monitoring and management to maintain the desired balance. This may involve periodically rebalancing the portfolio by selling assets that have performed well and buying those that have underperformed, which can lead to higher costs than initially estimated.

While diversification is an important strategy, there is the risk of overdiversification, where a portfolio becomes too diluted by holding too many different assets. This can lead to suboptimal performance and make managing the portfolio effectively more difficult. When discussing diversification as a fundamental investment requirement, it is essential to clarify that diversification is crucial up to the point where it becomes problematic. High costs, mediocre performance, and the complexity of managing an over-diversified portfolio are some of the difficulties that can arise when the effort to reduce risk leads to excessive asset purchases. Therefore, it is as important to diversify enough as it is to avoid over-diversification.

RISK VS. RETURN

The principle of risk vs. return is a fundamental concept in investing that indicates that higher risk generally comes with the potential for higher returns. Understanding this relationship is crucial for making informed investment decisions that align with an investor's financial goals and risk tolerance.

Risk is the possibility that the actual return on an investment will differ from the expected return, including the possibility of losing the invested capital. Risk can be caused by market, economic, political, or company-specific factors. In other words, it is the uncertainty associated with any investment and the probability that an investment will not meet the investor's expectations.

On the other hand, return is the gain or loss derived from an investment over a period of time. It is usually measured as a percentage of the invested capital and can include income from interest, dividends, and capital appreciation. Return is what investors expect to receive as compensation for assuming a certain level of risk.

There are several types of risks that can lead to partial or total loss of our investment. Considering the inherent risks in investing can help us better assess the suitability of an investment. When discussing risk, the goal is not to scare potential investors, but to ensure they have a comprehensive understanding of the challenges involved and approach investing with caution. Over time, investors will not only gain a better understanding of investment risks but also develop better tools to handle these challenges and protect their invested capital. Let's explore the different types of risks encountered in investing:

- Market Risk: Also known as systematic risk, market risk is related to overall market fluctuations that affect all assets. This type of risk cannot be eliminated through diversification. For example, an economic recession, a financial crisis, or changes in interest rates can negatively impact the value of investments in general. However, as discussed in the diversification section, we can minimize its impact by identifying different phases of the economic cycle and positioning ourselves in sectors or companies that handle certain phases of the cycle better than others.

- Specific Risk: Also known as unsystematic risk, specific risk is associated with a particular company or industry. This type of risk can be mitigated through portfolio diversification. For example, specific issues with a company, such as a management scandal or a failed product launch, can significantly affect the value of its stock.

- Inflation Risk: Inflation risk is the risk that inflation will erode the real value of investment returns. As discussed earlier, inflation reduces the purchasing power of money, meaning that nominal returns may not be sufficient to maintain the real value of an investment.

- Credit Risk: Credit risk is the possibility that a bond issuer will fail to pay interest or principal. This type of risk is particularly relevant for investors in corporate bonds and bonds from countries with low credit ratings. A default can result in significant losses for investors.

As we have seen, there are several risks that can erode our capital in the long journey of investing, and it is essential to take these risks into account when making investment decisions. One key to successful investing is finding the right balance between risk and return, aligned with the investor's financial goals and risk tolerance. To illustrate this, let's look at examples of two investors who, based on their profiles, might invest in different financial instruments.

- High-Risk, High-Return Investments: Individual growth stocks can provide substantial returns if the companies succeed, but they can also be very volatile and risky. Cryptocurrencies, with their high volatility and lack of regulation, represent another form of high-risk, high-return investment. Startups, while offering the potential for exponential returns, have a high failure rate. This investor might be willing to endure significant fluctuations in their portfolio's value in exchange for the potential for high returns. For example, they might invest in emerging technology stocks that have the potential to revolutionize the industry but also face a high likelihood of failure. Such investments are complex, as predicting the next successful company is challenging, and maintaining the investment over long periods while dealing with significant price fluctuations can be difficult.

- Low-Risk, Low-Return Investments: This category includes government bonds, savings accounts, and certificates of deposit. These investments are safer but offer more modest returns. Government bonds are backed by the trust and credit of the issuing government, making them less risky. Savings accounts and certificates of deposit are insured, providing additional security to the invested capital. A conservative investor might prefer a larger proportion of government bonds and bond funds, accepting lower returns in exchange for greater security. This investor values capital preservation and seeks a stable, predictable source of income. For example, they might invest in U.S. Treasury bonds, considered low risk due to the country's economic stability. However, this type of investment can be frustrating over time as returns may barely exceed inflation, which, as we have seen, erodes purchasing power. Although seemingly simple and calm, this type of investment may not yield the desired results, and capital appreciation may be lower than desired.

While, in the world of investing, there are usually no purely aggressive investors or purely conservative ones, and certainly none positioned at such extremes, the two previous examples were meant to give us an idea of the type of investor that exists at each end of the investment spectrum. The truth is that each investor must find a balance between achieving their desired returns and, at the same time, having the peace of mind of knowing their money is invested. There are two fundamental recommendations that can guide investors who are entering the world of investing for the first time.

If the investor is young, they can take on a more aggressive approach when investing. The smaller amount of capital invested, along with the possibility of correcting mistakes in the coming years, gives younger people more room to be aggressive in their investments. On the other hand, individuals who have been investing for a while and have accumulated a significant amount of capital should adopt a more conservative approach, where their main goal should be to preserve the capital they have already gained.

Another recommendation is to start in the investment world with a more conservative approach. The first years of an investor are the most challenging, where most mistakes are made, and where, little by little, they discover the area of investing in which they feel most comfortable. Over time, this approach may gradually change. Experience, as well as the knowledge acquired over time, allows the investor to have greater analytical capacity and take on riskier investments.

These two pieces of advice may seem contradictory since younger investors can afford to be more aggressive, but at the same time, if it's their first years investing, they should maintain a more conservative approach. It's simply about finding a balance between these two variables: the investor's age and their investment experience, always keeping in mind that money needs time and patience to grow, so we must be careful with the investment strategies we use.

TIME HORIZON

The investment horizon is an essential concept in financial planning, referring to the period of time an investor expects to hold an investment before needing access to the funds. This factor is crucial because it directly influences asset selection and investment strategy. Understanding and defining the investment horizon helps align financial decisions with short-, medium-, and long-term goals.

   - Short-Term: Short-term investments are those held for a period of up to three years. In this horizon, the priority is capital security and liquidity, as the investor may need to access the funds in the near future. Investments should be relatively safe to minimize the risk of significant losses. Typical examples include high-yield savings accounts, short-term certificates of deposit (CDs), and treasury bonds with near-term maturities.

   Short-term investments are more suitable for immediate financial goals, such as maintaining an emergency fund to cover unexpected situations. Due to the need for accessibility and safety, these investments often focus on liquid, low-risk assets. High-yield savings accounts provide a safe place to park money while earning a modest return. Short-term bonds and money market funds are also viable options, offering stability and liquidity.

   - Medium-Term: Medium-term investments are those held from three to ten years. This horizon allows for a greater tolerance for risk compared to the short term, offering potential for higher returns. Investors in this category may consider a mix of medium-term bonds, money market funds, and some low-risk stocks or mutual funds. This horizon is suitable for financial goals such as buying a house, funding a child's education, or purchasing a vehicle.

   For a medium-term investment horizon, investors can take on slightly more risk compared to the short term, seeking a balance between security and growth. Medium-term bonds offer higher returns than short-term bonds and are less volatile than stocks. Mutual funds and exchange-traded funds (ETFs) that diversify across multiple sectors are also appropriate, providing moderate growth with manageable risk. Even within this time frame, investors can begin to build a portfolio that includes stable company stocks.

- Long-Term: Long-term investments refer to those held for more than ten years. Long-term investors can tolerate more volatility with the expectation that markets will recover and provide solid returns over time. This horizon is ideal for goals such as retirement or financial independence, where compounding interest and capital appreciation can be maximized. Investment options include stocks, mutual funds, real estate, and long-term bonds.

For those who choose stocks as their primary investment vehicle, the time horizon should be as long as possible, with a minimum recommendation of at least three years and ideally over ten years. This extended horizon allows volatility and economic cycles to dissipate over time, preventing investors from selling at the worst market moments, which would be a significant error.

TYPES OF INVESTMENTS

There are numerous instruments to invest and monetize our savings. These range from more conservative instruments, such as high-yield savings accounts or short-term government bonds that can be held to maturity, to more aggressive instruments, such as cyclical stocks or cryptocurrency investments. However, historically, it has been proven year after year that when our investment horizon is long-term, i.e. beyond 10 years, there is no excuse for not choosing stocks as the main type of investment.

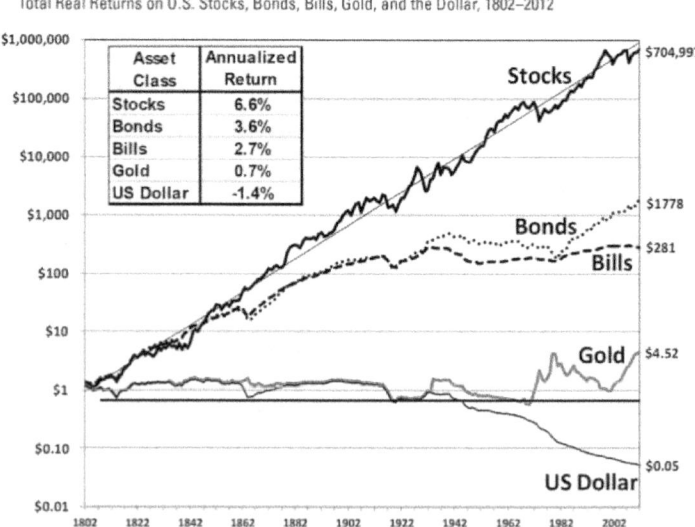

Total Real Returns on U.S. Stocks, Bonds, Bills, Gold, and the Dollar, 1802–2012

As shown in the previous chart, for over 200 years, stocks have been the financial instrument that has significantly outperformed others in terms of returns for investors. This makes it obvious to recommend investing in this type of product when the time horizon is long-term. However, several nuances need to be considered regarding this assertion.

Firstly, the chart refers to North American stocks, which have been exceptionally profitable compared to other global stock markets. It's important to note that this performance may not be representative of all international markets.

Secondly, the figures are presented in US dollars, while investors from other countries, such as Spain, operate in their local currencies, like the euro. This introduces significant variation due to exchange rate fluctuations.

Thirdly, the inflation considered in these charts is US inflation, which may differ considerably from that experienced in other countries, affecting the real return on investments.

Fourthly, it's necessary to consider the evolution of markets and investor participation. Since 2009, stock markets, especially in the US, have shown sustained growth, coinciding with the rise of passive or indexed management.

Lastly, and most importantly, something that affects all investors regardless of geographic location is that there have been periods of many years where returns have been insufficient, which can test the patience of even the most stoic investors. An investment made at the beginning of 2001 would have taken 15 years to recover. An investment made in 2002 would have needed 13 years, and those from 2003-2004 would have taken between 9 and 10 years. These periods are significant. For an investor close to retirement, facing a market like that of 2000-2002 or 2000-2008 could result in a loss of 50% or more of their accumulated capital, drastically altering their return expectations and withdrawal plans.

It is true that this example is extreme and could be considered biased, but even under favorable conditions, the time required to recover from a significant market decline often exceeds 5 years. This case, though extreme, highlights the importance of considering risks, market variations, and realistic expectations for recovery. Diversification and patience are essential for effectively managing investments and mitigating the negative impacts of market fluctuations.

STOCKS

Stocks represent a share in the ownership of a company and are one of the most common and accessible forms of investment in modern financial markets. By purchasing stocks, investors become shareholders and gain rights to a portion of the company's assets and profits. This concept, while simple in essence, is fundamental to the operation of capitalism and the global economy. Stocks are traded on stock exchanges, such as the New York Stock Exchange (NYSE) and Nasdaq, where millions of transactions occur daily, moving trillions of dollars and reflecting the state of the economy.

When buying stocks, investors acquire a fraction of the company's ownership. This not only means owning a proportional part of the company's assets, but also gaining certain rights, such as the right to vote at shareholder meetings. These votes can influence important decisions, such as the election of the board of directors and the approval of corporate policies. Being a shareholder grants individuals a voice in the company's future, although the weight of that voice depends on the number of shares owned.

Some companies choose to distribute a portion of their profits to shareholders in the form of dividends. These payments can be quarterly, semi-annual, or annual and represent a source of passive income for investors. Dividends are particularly attractive to investors seeking regular income, such as retirees. Not all companies pay dividends; some prefer to reinvest their profits into growth and expansion or through share buybacks, which are often the most efficient way to allocate resources when the company's growth potential is exhausted.

Additionally, investors can benefit from the appreciation of stock prices. If a company performs well and its stock value increases, shareholders can sell their shares at a higher price than the purchase price, realizing a capital gain. Capital appreciation is one of the main reasons people invest in stocks, as it allows for wealth accumulation over time.

Advantages of Investing in Stocks:

As seen in the previous chart, historically, stocks have provided higher returns compared to other types of investments, such as bonds and savings accounts. This ability to generate high returns makes them attractive to investors seeking to maximize long-term capital growth. Stories of success from investors who have made fortunes investing in stocks are numerous and well-documented, from the early days of Wall Street to recent surges in technology companies' value.

Another significant advantage of stocks is their high liquidity. Stocks can be bought and sold easily on the stock market, allowing investors to quickly convert their investments into cash if needed. This ease of transaction is crucial for investors who may need to access their money in the short term due to emergencies or changes in financial circumstances. However, as mentioned several times, the ideal scenario in stock investing would be to keep the capital invested for long periods.

Disadvantages of Investing in Stocks:

The value of stocks can fluctuate significantly due to economic, political, and company-specific factors. Economic recessions, changes in government policies, wars, and other macroeconomic events can cause large variations in stock prices. This volatility can be unsettling for investors, especially for those who have a low risk tolerance or are new to investing.

Additionally, if a company faces financial difficulties, its stock value can decrease drastically. This can occur due to poor management, changes in the industry, loss of competitive advantages, or any disruption of internal and external factors. Investors should be aware that even well-established companies are not immune to problems, and it is possible to lose part or all of the investment if a company goes bankrupt.

Research and Analysis:

To invest in stocks, it is essential to understand fundamental aspects of the company, both qualitatively and quantitatively. Investing in a company because it is trendy, has dropped significantly, or is rising sharply, is like choosing a number at random in a casino roulette. In the investment world, we should aim to eliminate as much uncertainty and chance as possible and lay the groundwork for a higher probability of success.

Therefore, conducting thorough research and analysis of the company is crucial for making informed investment decisions. This includes analyzing financial statements, evaluating competitors, studying market trends, and staying updated with economic and political news. Well-informed investors are better equipped to identify investment opportunities and avoid potential pitfalls.

The goal of fundamental analysis is to determine a stock's intrinsic value and compare it to the current market price. If the intrinsic value is higher than the market price, the stock could be a good buy. Below is a detailed guide on how to conduct fundamental analysis of a company.

Understanding the Company's Business:

This is the first step and involves analyzing how the company makes money, what its main products or services are, and what competitive advantages it possesses. A good understanding of the business model is crucial for assessing the company's long-term potential.

Moreover, it's important to place the company within the context of its industry. This includes analyzing the competitive environment, barriers to entry, market trends, and the company's position in the industry. Tools such as Porter's Five Forces analysis can be useful here.

Financial Statement Analysis:

On the other hand, we need to examine the three main financial statements provided by the company annually: the balance sheet, the income statement, and the cash flow statement.

The balance sheet provides a snapshot of the company's assets, liabilities, and equity at a specific point in time. Assets include cash, accounts receivable, inventories, and property, plant, and equipment. Liabilities include accounts payable, short-term and long-term debts. Finally, equity represents the difference between assets and liabilities, reflecting the shareholders' stake in the company.

The income statement shows the company's revenues and expenses over a specific period, revealing its profitability. Revenues provide information about the net sales generated from the company's products or services. Expenses include the cost of goods sold, operating expenses, interest expenses, and taxes. The net income shows the revenue minus expenses, representing the company's net profit.

Lastly, the cash flow statement provides information on the cash generated and used by the company in three areas: operations, investing, and financing. Operating cash flow determines the cash generated from regular business operations. Investing cash flow represents the cash used to buy or sell long-term assets. Financing cash flow shows the cash received or paid through financing activities, such as issuing stock or repaying debt.

Financial Ratios Evaluation

The function of financial ratios is to diagnose the company's finances to assess its financial balance, profitability, and financial independence.

Profitability ratios measure the company's ability to generate profit. For example:
- Gross Profit Margin: (Revenue - Cost of Goods Sold) / Revenue.
- Operating Profit Margin: Operating Profit / Revenue.
- Net Profit Margin: Net Profit / Revenue.
- ROE (Return on Equity): Net Profit / Equity.
- ROA (Return on Assets): Net Profit / Total Assets.

Liquidity ratios evaluate the company's ability to meet short-term obligations. This is important as analyzing these ratios can give an idea of whether the company might go bankrupt in the short term. Common liquidity ratios include:
- Current Ratio: Current Assets / Current Liabilities.
- Quick Ratio: (Current Assets - Inventories) / Current Liabilities.

Debt ratios measure the company's level of debt relative to its equity or assets. Like liquidity ratios, they help assess the financial health of the company and can indicate potential risks due to high levels of debt. Key debt ratios are:
- Debt-to-Equity Ratio: Total Debt / Equity.
- Debt-to-Assets Ratio: Total Debt / Total Assets.

Efficiency ratios analyze how effectively the company uses its resources, providing insight into its ability to generate income with available resources. Examples include:
- Inventory Turnover: Cost of Goods Sold / Average Inventory.
- Receivables Turnover: Net Sales / Average Accounts Receivable.
- Asset Turnover: Revenue / Total Assets.

Qualitative Analysis:

Qualitative analysis is as important, if not more so, than quantitative analysis. Through qualitative analysis, we can understand why a company achieves the results it does and judge whether certain competitive advantages are sustainable over time.

To start, we should analyze the business model, which refers to how a company generates profit with a product. A business model encompasses all aspects involved in designing the solutions a business offers, considering the contribution of products, goods, or services to the quality of life of consumers.

Additionally, we should analyze the competitive advantages of the company in which we wish to invest. A competitive advantage includes all aspects and characteristics that make a brand or product stand out from the competition.

Naturally, there are various competitive advantages, such as cost leadership, product differentiation, and one of the most important concepts in studying competitive advantages: the cost of switching. The cost of switching refers to the barriers a company puts in place to discourage customers from changing suppliers, either directly or indirectly. For example, consider Microsoft Excel, a widely used tool. Switching to another program would not only involve adapting all company files but also training employees and facing inefficiencies in sharing information with other companies still using Excel. Most companies prefer to stick with the program and continue paying, even with price increases, rather than switching to a new supplier.

It's also important to analyze the management team of the company. The management team should not only be efficient in managing the company's resources but ideally, they should be shareholders who share the company's fortunes with other investors. This concept is known as "skin in the game," a term from English that literally translates to "skin in the game" and specifically refers to the direct involvement of company executives in a project or investment by funding a portion with their own money. "Skin in the game" ensures alignment of interests between investors with shares and executives managing the company's capital. By investing their own money and putting their own "skin in the game," alongside investors, the likelihood of fraud and financial mismanagement is reduced.

Finally, we should analyze factors such as the growth of the company's sector, as well as potential tailwinds and headwinds that may appear in the coming years. If the company we invest in has competitive advantages, is managed by a team with "skin in the game," operates in a sector with favorable future trends, and is at least reasonably priced, we will have improved our chances of success in the world of investing.

To understand the last point, it is essential to know the company's value. Here, we provide guidelines for tackling the significant challenge of calculating a company's intrinsic value. It goes without saying that, in addition to being more complicated than what can be explained in a few pages, calculating intrinsic value is often more of an art than an exact science.

Company Valuation:

To value a company, we can use two types of valuations. First, and the most common, is relative valuation, where market multiples are used to compare the company's valuation with its competitors. The main advantage of this valuation method is its simplicity, as it requires very little time to perform, and in most cases, the information can be easily found online.

However, it has several disadvantages. One drawback is that each company is unique, and by comparing ratios with other companies in the sector, we assume that their characteristics are similar, which may not be the case. To address this, we must understand factors like competitive advantages, growth, etc., to ensure we are comparing similar companies. Even with this understanding, we cannot be 100% sure that different companies analyzed and compared using these multiples should trade at the same level.

Another difficulty is that using multiples can overlook the company's future. For example, imagine a company trading at a multiple that seems very cheap, making it an attractive opportunity, but we haven't done the proper qualitative analysis and are unaware that the company is at a production peak or facing a challenging situation. What initially seemed cheap may eventually turn out to be expensive and one of our worst investments.

Therefore, when analyzing a company, we must consider all the previously mentioned variables (business model, financial statements, financial ratios, qualitative analysis, and company valuation). Only after analyzing these aspects can we determine with some certainty the suitability of the investment.

The most common and widely used multiples for valuation are:

P/E (Price/Earnings) Ratio or PER: Stock Price / Earnings Per Share.

P/B (Price/Book) Ratio: Stock Price / Book Value Per Share (especially for insurance and banking companies).

EV/EBITDA (Enterprise Value/EBITDA): Enterprise Value / EBITDA.

EV/FCF (Enterprise Value/FCF): Enterprise Value / Free Cash Flow (the multiple that best reflects the reality of the company being analyzed).

In addition to relative valuation, intrinsic valuation uses the discounted cash flow method. This is a much more complex valuation as it requires knowledge of the company's financial statements, projecting them into the future (3 to 5 years), then discounting them to calculate their present value. This present value is compared with the company's market price, allowing us to understand whether the company is priced attractively or not.

As with the previous method, intrinsic valuation has its advantages and disadvantages. The main advantage is that developing discounted cash flow models and projecting balance sheet items, as well as the income statement and cash flow statement, helps us better understand the company, not just in quantitative terms but also in important qualitative aspects.

However, its main disadvantage is the difficulty in projecting cash flows and, particularly, in determining what is known as terminal value. This terminal value corresponds to the value we assign to the company from the last year of projection (3 or 5 years) and significantly affects the final result of the model. The terminal value should be higher for growth companies and lower for stable and established companies. This is because growth companies are expected to continue growing at high levels beyond the projected 3 or 5 years, while stable companies will have slower growth. This makes valuing a high-growth company more complex than valuing mature and stable companies, as the terminal value is easier to determine for the latter.

Unfortunately, this book will not go into more detail on discounted cash flow models, as that would require a whole book on the subject.

Continuous Monitoring:

Buying a stock is just the beginning of the investment process. As you will understand, the investment process is not a one-time event but a continuous effort that requires constant monitoring and analysis. Monitoring the performance of the invested company, as well as changes in market conditions, is essential to protect and maximize the value of the investment. Regular review of financial statements, analyst reports, and relevant news is crucial to ensure that the original investment thesis remains valid and adapts to new market realities.

Imagine an investor who has invested in a technology company due to its strong position in the artificial intelligence (AI) market. The investment thesis is based on the expectation that demand for AI technologies will continue to grow rapidly in the coming years, driving revenue and profit growth for the company.

After buying the company's stock, the investor must periodically review the company's financial statements to ensure it is meeting its growth projections. Analyst reports can provide additional insights into the AI sector's outlook and how the company compares with its competitors. Additionally, it is crucial to stay updated on developments in technology, regulatory changes, and any other factors that could impact the demand for AI technologies.

If, during one of these periodic reviews, the investor discovers that the company is losing market share to a new competitor with superior technology or that new regulations are imposing significant restrictions on AI applications, this might indicate that the original investment thesis is no longer valid. In such cases, the investor will need to make informed decisions about whether to maintain the investment, adjust the strategy, or sell the position.

After purchasing a stock, a long road awaits, where monitoring investments, rebalancing portfolios, and dealing with crises are essential. Stock investors must be aware of their active role. In the following pages, we will see how this role can become less active if we choose to invest in other financial instruments that, due to their characteristics, require less of our attention and are suitable for those who do not want to spend as much time on the investment process.

BONDS

Bonds are one of the oldest and most essential investment instruments in the financial world. They represent a form of loan where the investor, by purchasing a bond, lends money to an issuing entity, which can be a government, a corporation, or an institution. In return, the issuer commits to repaying the principal amount at the bond's maturity and making periodic interest payments, known as coupons.

To understand how bonds work, we need to grasp the following three concepts. First, the coupon of a bond, which is the periodic interest payment the issuer makes to the investor. Coupons can be fixed-rate, where the interest payment is constant over time, or variable-rate, where the payment can fluctuate based on a benchmark, such as a market interest rate. Second, we need to understand the maturity of a bond, which is the date when the issuer must return the face value to the investor. Bonds can have maturity periods ranging from a few months to several decades. Maturity periods often influence the level of risk and return of the bond. Finally, the face value, also known as par value, is the amount the issuer agrees to pay the investor at the bond's maturity. Typically, the face value is the initial amount the investor lends to the issuer.

When investing in bonds, we can choose between government bonds, corporate bonds (issued by companies), and municipal bonds. Government bonds are issued by national and local governments, such as U.S. Treasury bonds, and are generally considered low-risk due to the government's ability to raise taxes and print money to meet its obligations. However, the returns on these bonds are usually lower compared to other types of bonds due to their lower risk. Corporate bonds are issued by companies to finance their operations and projects. These bonds tend to offer higher returns than government bonds due to their higher risk level. The financial health of the issuing company is a crucial factor in evaluating these bonds, and before investing, we must thoroughly understand the company's economic and financial situation. Lastly, municipal bonds are issued by local governments, such as states, municipalities, and other public entities, to finance projects like roads, schools, and hospitals. A significant advantage of municipal bonds is that the interest paid may be exempt from federal taxes and sometimes state and local taxes, making them attractive to investors in high tax brackets.

However, before investing in bonds, we should be aware of some of their advantages and disadvantages, as they are often overlooked, assuming that the level of risk is low or non-existent, which is not always the case.

One of the main advantages of bonds is that they provide regular interest payments, offering a predictable income stream. This is especially attractive for investors seeking stability and consistency in their income, such as retirees or those with a low tolerance for risk. Additionally, compared to stocks, although this is not always the case, bonds generally exhibit lower volatility. This is due to the predictable nature of their interest payments and the return of principal at maturity. As a result, bonds are a preferred option for conservative investors looking to preserve their capital.

On the other hand, it is important to highlight the main disadvantages or risks associated with investing in bonds. Credit risk is the possibility that the bond issuer may fail to meet interest payments or repay the principal. This risk is higher in corporate and municipal bonds compared to government bonds. The issuer's creditworthiness is assessed through credit ratings provided by agencies such as Moody's, Standard & Poor's, and Fitch. One of the lesser-known disadvantages is interest rate risk. The value of bonds in the secondary market can fluctuate inversely with changes in interest rates. When interest rates rise, the price of existing bonds tends to fall, and vice versa. This risk is particularly relevant for investors who might need to sell their bonds before maturity. For example, imagine we have invested in a 10-year bond, and due to exceptional circumstances, we need to access the invested money earlier. There is a secondary market where these bonds can be transferred, but the value of the bonds will depend on several factors such as interest rate changes and the issuer's credit quality. As a result, we might find that the value of our bonds in the secondary market is lower than the original value. Therefore, we should not be misled when bonds are categorized as fixed-income securities, as their value can vary over time. It is safest to hold these bonds until maturity to avoid potential losses in the secondary market.

Bond Investment Process:

Before investing in bonds, it is crucial for investors to assess their risk profile. This includes considering their risk tolerance, time horizon, and income needs, as discussed in previous chapters. Conservative investors may prefer government bonds or high-rated municipal bonds, while those with a higher risk tolerance may opt for high-yield corporate bonds.

Once the risk profile is defined, investors should select the appropriate bonds. This involves analyzing the bond's characteristics, such as the coupon, maturity, and face value, as well as the issuer's creditworthiness. Diversification is also a key strategy for managing risk, distributing investments across different issuers and sectors.

Bonds can be purchased in the primary market, directly from the issuer at the time of issuance, or in the secondary market, where existing bonds are traded among investors. Bond brokers and online investment platforms are common means to purchase bonds.

Finally, after purchasing bonds, it is essential to regularly monitor their performance and market conditions. Investors should stay alert to changes in interest rates, the financial health of the issuer, and other macroeconomic factors that could affect the value of their bond investments.

Bond Investment Strategies:

Without delving too deeply into complex concepts, here are some key strategies for investing in bonds:

1. Buy and Hold to Maturity Strategy: This strategy involves purchasing bonds and holding them until maturity, receiving periodic interest payments and the principal amount at the end. It is suitable for investors seeking stability and predictable returns.

2. Barbell Strategy: This strategy consists of investing in bonds with short-term and long-term maturities while avoiding intermediate-term bonds. This approach allows investors to benefit from higher interest rates on long-term bonds while maintaining flexibility with short-term bonds.

3. Laddering Strategy: Laddering is a strategy where investors purchase bonds with different maturity dates. As short-term bonds mature, the funds are reinvested in new long-term bonds. This strategy helps manage interest rate risk and provides a steady stream of income.

REAL ESTATE

Real estate investment is a financial strategy that involves acquiring properties with the goal of generating income and/or appreciating capital over time. This type of investment covers a broad range of properties, including residential homes, commercial buildings, land, and industrial properties. Throughout history, real estate has been a popular avenue for wealth creation due to its potential to provide stable income and capital appreciation.

On one hand, residential properties include houses, apartments, and condominiums. These properties are commonly purchased with the intention of renting them out to tenants or reselling them at a higher price in the future. Investing in residential properties can be an excellent way to generate passive income, as rental payments provide a steady stream of monthly income. Additionally, residential properties can appreciate in value over time, especially in areas with high demand for housing.

On the other hand, commercial properties include offices, retail spaces, and shopping centers used for business activities. Investing in commercial properties can offer higher returns due to the elevated rents paid by businesses. However, this type of investment may require significant initial capital and active management to keep the property in optimal condition and ensure high-quality tenants.

Lastly, industrial properties include factories, warehouses, and land designated for industrial use. This type of investment is attractive for those seeking stable, long-term income, as industrial properties often have long-term lease agreements with manufacturing, logistics, and storage companies. Industrial properties can also offer tax advantages and less competition compared to residential and commercial properties.

As mentioned earlier, the primary advantages of investing in real estate include the ability to generate consistent income through rent. Property owners can obtain stable monthly income by renting their properties to residential or commercial tenants. This passive income stream can be particularly appealing for those looking to diversify their income sources and secure regular revenue. Additionally, properties can increase in value over time, providing significant benefits upon sale. Capital appreciation is the difference between the initial purchase price of the property and its current market value. This increase in value can result in a substantial profit for the investor when they decide to sell the property. Capital appreciation can be influenced by factors such as urban development, infrastructure improvements, and economic growth in the region. Finally, investing in real estate can act as a diversification tool in an investment portfolio. Real estate tends to have a low correlation with other financial assets, such as stocks and bonds. This means that property values may not fluctuate in the same way as stock markets, offering protection against financial market volatility.

However, it is important to note that investing in real estate has significant barriers to entry. On one hand, a high amount of capital is required to purchase property, making it inaccessible to all investors who want to start investing. On the other hand, real estate investment often involves a lack of liquidity. Selling a property can take time, and finding buyers quickly is not always easy. Unlike stocks or bonds, which can be sold within days, the sale of real estate can take months or even years. This lack of liquidity can be a problem for investors who need to access their capital quickly. Additionally, property owners must cover maintenance costs, repairs, and property taxes. These costs can accumulate quickly and impact the net returns of the investment, not to mention the possibility of facing unexpected expenses, such as emergency repairs or necessary renovations to keep the property attractive to tenants.

Another aspect to consider when investing in real estate is that property values can fluctuate due to economic and real estate market factors. Economic changes, such as recessions or increases in interest rates, can negatively affect property values. Moreover, real estate market conditions, such as oversupply or decreased demand in a specific region, can impact property prices. Investors need to be aware of these risks and develop strategies to mitigate their effects.

Lastly, potential risks include tenant defaults and possible occupation of the property—a risk increasingly common in many countries where legislation tends to establish barriers to recovering an occupied property.

Real Estate Investment Process:

The first step in real estate investment is conducting thorough research to identify properties that align with the investor's goals. This includes analyzing the local real estate market, evaluating the potential for capital appreciation, and considering the rental income that the property can generate. It is crucial to assess the property's location, as areas with high housing demand or commercial development tend to offer better investment opportunities.

Once a property is selected, the next step is to perform a detailed financial evaluation. This involves calculating the expected return on investment, considering rental income, maintenance costs, and potential increases in property value. Investors should also account for acquisition costs, such as real estate agent fees, closing costs, and taxes.

Additionally, financing is a crucial part of the real estate investment process. Investors may use various methods to finance their acquisitions, such as mortgages, private loans, or partnerships with other investors. It is important to ensure that the financing terms are favorable and sustainable in the long term.

Finally, effective property management is essential to maximize investment returns. This includes selecting suitable tenants, maintaining the property, and managing finances. Property owners can choose to manage the property themselves or hire a property management company to handle these responsibilities.

Real Estate Investment Strategies:

1. Buy and Rent: The buy-and-rent strategy involves acquiring properties to rent them out to residential or commercial tenants. This strategy

provides a steady flow of rental income and can result in long-term capital appreciation. It is ideal for investors seeking passive income and who are willing to manage properties.

2. Rehabilitation and Sale: Also known as "fix and flip," this strategy involves buying properties that need repairs, renovating them, and selling them at a higher price. This approach can generate significant profits in a short period of time but requires knowledge of renovations and a deep understanding of the local real estate market.

3. Real Estate Development: Real estate development involves purchasing land and constructing new properties. This strategy can be highly profitable, but also comes with a high level of risk and requires a significantly larger capital investment compared to other investment strategies. Developers require experience in construction, planning, and permits to succeed in this strategy.

4. Commercial Real Estate Investment: Similar to the previously mentioned strategy, investing in commercial properties, such as offices and shopping centers, requires a substantial investment but can offer high returns due to the high rents paid by businesses. It is suitable for investors with experience and significant capital.

For investors who have dismissed this type of investment due to the high capital required, it is good to know that there are instruments such as REITs (Real Estate Investment Trusts). Real Estate Investment Trusts (REITs) are investment funds that own and operate income-generating real estate. These can include a wide range of properties, such as shopping centers, offices, apartments, hospitals, hotels, and other types of real estate. REITs allow investors to access the real estate market without having to buy and manage properties directly. REITs must comply with certain regulations, such as distributing at least 90% of their taxable income to shareholders in the form of dividends. This makes them an attractive source of regular income for investors who want to invest in real estate but do not have substantial capital. Investing in a REIT is as simple as buying its shares, just like any other company, with the only difference being the business sector the company operates in.

INVESTMENT FUNDS

Investment funds are financial vehicles that allow multiple investors to pool their money to invest in a variety of assets, such as stocks, bonds, and other financial instruments. These funds are managed by professionals who make investment decisions on behalf of the investors. Investment funds offer instant diversification and are a popular option for both novice and experienced investors looking to manage risk and maximize returns.

Types of Investment Funds:

1. Mutual Funds: Mutual funds are actively managed by professionals who select securities with the aim of outperforming the market. Fund managers constantly analyze the market and adjust portfolios to capitalize on investment opportunities. Mutual funds can invest in a wide range of assets, including stocks, bonds, and other financial instruments. Their main advantage is active management, which can potentially lead to higher returns and greater diversification. However, this comes with higher management fees and the risk of not beating the market.

2. Index Funds: Index funds are passively managed and designed to replicate the performance of a specific market index, such as the S&P 500, which consists of the 500 largest companies in the U.S. These funds invest in the same securities that make up the index and maintain a similar composition over time. Index funds offer a simple and low-cost way for investors to gain exposure to an entire market or sector. Their main advantage is simplicity, as they are ideal for those who want to achieve returns similar to an index without the complexities and detailed analysis required for investing in individual stocks. Conversely, their main disadvantage may be less flexibility, as investments are made in pre-built stock packages, and returns are limited to the performance of the index. Although this might seem like a significant disadvantage, it is worth noting that very few investors have consistently outperformed the market throughout history. Thus, what appears to be a disadvantage can quickly turn into a non-issue, if not an advantage.

3. Money Market Funds: Money market funds invest in short-term, high-quality debt instruments, such as Treasury bills and certificates of deposit. These funds are known for offering high liquidity and safety, making them suitable for investors seeking to preserve capital and earn modest income. They are more conservative than the previously mentioned funds, with the main advantage being high liquidity, low risk, and stability. However, as conservative instruments, they typically offer lower expected returns.

Investment Process in Investment Funds:

Before investing in investment funds, it is crucial to clearly define investment objectives. This includes determining the investment horizon, the level of risk tolerance, and specific financial goals.

The next step is to research and select the investment funds that best align with the defined objectives. This involves analyzing the fund's historical performance, associated fees and expenses, investment strategy, and the reputation of the fund manager. Investors can use online resources, analysis reports, and professional financial advice to make informed decisions.

Additionally, it is important to understand all the fees and expenses associated with investment funds. This includes management fees, administrative expenses, and any purchase or sales commissions. Fees can have a significant impact on long-term returns, so selecting funds with competitive cost structures is crucial.

Investment Strategies in Investment Funds

1. Systematic Investment: Systematic investment, or Dollar-Cost Averaging (DCA), is a strategy where investors buy a fixed amount of investment funds at regular intervals, regardless of the price. This strategy helps mitigate market risk by averaging the cost of investments over time and can reduce the impact of market volatility.

2. Regular Rebalancing: Regular rebalancing of the portfolio is a strategy where investors adjust their investment composition to maintain the desired asset allocation. This may involve selling funds that have significantly increased in value and buying more of those that have decreased, ensuring that the portfolio remains aligned with investment goals and risk profile. Rebalancing should be done periodically, considering associated costs, and thus should not be performed too frequently but rather as a medium-term objective.

ETFs

Exchange-Traded Funds (ETFs) offer investors various forms of diversification and access to a wide range of assets. These instruments have become increasingly popular due to their flexibility, accessibility, and low costs, providing additional options beyond traditional investments in stocks and bonds.

ETFs are traded on stock exchanges in the same way as individual stocks. This means investors can buy and sell ETFs during market hours, offering greater flexibility and liquidity compared to other types of investment funds. This feature facilitates entering and exiting positions, which is especially useful for investors looking to capitalize on market fluctuations.

One of the main advantages of ETFs is their ability to provide instant diversification. ETFs can track a wide variety of indices, sectors, commodities, and other assets. For example, an ETF may follow the performance of a market index like the S&P 500, a specific sector like technology, or a commodity like gold. This allows investors to access a broad spectrum of assets with a single investment.

Moreover, ETFs generally have lower costs than actively managed mutual funds. This is because most ETFs are passively managed, involving less intervention from the fund manager and therefore lower management fees. Lower costs can translate into higher net returns for investors over the long term.

Undoubtedly, ETFs become a fundamental instrument for those who want to achieve the returns associated with stock investments but in a more diversified and cost-effective manner. They are recommended for investors who lack the time or knowledge to invest in individual stocks but wish to benefit from the returns offered by such products.

CHAPTER 2:
INVESTMENT STRATEGIES

VALUE INVESTING

Value investing is an investment strategy focused on buying stocks that the market has undervalued relative to their intrinsic value. This approach was popularized by Benjamin Graham and David Dodd in their book Security Analysis and later by Warren Buffett, one of the most successful investors of all time.

As previously discussed, intrinsic value is an estimate of a company's true worth based on its financial fundamentals and long-term growth potential. Value investors seek companies whose market price is below this intrinsic value, indicating a buying opportunity.

To be a successful value investor, it is essential to understand several key concepts. One of the most important is fundamental analysis. This involves examining a company's financial statements, including its balance sheet, income statement, and cash flow statement. Value investors look for companies with strong fundamentals, such as stable revenues, low debt levels, and healthy cash flow.

Another fundamental concept is the margin of safety. Introduced by Benjamin Graham, this concept refers to the difference between a company's intrinsic value and its market price. A higher margin of safety provides extra protection against miscalculations and market fluctuations, so it is advisable to buy a stock when its margin of safety is as large as possible.

Moreover, to be a value investor, it is preferable to have a long-term investment perspective. Investors who adopt this viewpoint believe that the market will eventually recognize the true value of undervalued companies. This requires patience and discipline to maintain investments over time.

Identifying undervalued stocks requires careful analysis and the application of several financial and qualitative criteria. Here are some of the main criteria used by value investors:

1. Price-to-Earnings Ratio (P/E Ratio): The P/E ratio compares a stock's price to the company's earnings per share. A low P/E ratio may

suggest that a stock is undervalued, especially if the company has a solid track record of revenue and profit growth. It is important to compare the P/E ratio with the industry average and the company's historical P/E ratio.

2. Enterprise Value to Free Cash Flow (EV/FCF): This ratio compares a company's value with its free cash flow, which is the cash generated by a company after necessary capital expenditures to maintain or expand its assets. Value investors look for companies with a low EV/FCF ratio, as this can indicate a strong ability to generate cash that can be used to pay down debt, reinvest in the business, or return capital to shareholders.

3. Dividend Yield: The dividend yield is the annual dividend paid by a company divided by its stock price. A high dividend yield can indicate an undervalued stock, especially if the company has a history of consistent and sustainable dividend payments.

4. Revenue and Earnings Growth: Although value investing focuses on the current value, future growth is also important. Investors seek companies with a solid history of revenue and earnings growth, as well as a clear potential for continuing that growth.

5. Management Evaluation: The quality of a company's management is crucial. Value investors analyze the experience, vision, and ethics of the management team, as well as their track record of creating value for shareholders.

GROWTH INVESTING

While we view value investing and growth investing as "two sides of the same coin," we have decided to address them separately because it's common in the investment world to discuss each strategy individually. A good investor should consider both price factors and company growth factors, rather than isolating these variables. However, it is usual to categorize certain investors as either value or growth based on the profile of the companies in their portfolios, which is why we have decided to create separate sections for each strategy.

That said, growth investing is a strategy focused on investing in companies that are expected to grow at a rate faster than the market average. Growth investors seek companies with strong potential for expanding revenue, profits, and market value. Unlike value investing, which seeks undervalued companies, growth investing prioritizes future growth potential.

To be a successful growth investor, one must focus on finding growing companies and analyze several variables. First, it is essential to look for companies that are increasing their revenues at a significant rate. Rapid revenue growth suggests increasing demand for the company's products or services. In addition to revenue, profit growth is crucial. Companies must demonstrate the ability to convert their revenues into sustainable profits. Growth investors have a particular preference for innovative companies with disruptive products or services and a clear competitive advantage. Additionally, growing companies often reinvest a large portion of their earnings into business expansion, research and development, and/or marketing. This reinvestment is a positive indicator of their commitment to long-term growth. Finally, growth investing requires evaluating the market size and growth potential of the sector in which the company operates. Emerging and rapidly expanding sectors are particularly attractive.

As we see, finding companies with high growth potential requires a detailed analysis of various financial and qualitative factors:

- Revenue Growth Rate: Analyze the company's revenue growth history. A high compound annual growth rate (CAGR) in revenues is a positive indicator.

- Future Projections: Evaluate the company's future revenue growth projections. Analyst estimates and the company's own forecasts can provide insight into its growth potential.

- Profit Margin Expansion: Companies with growth potential should show an expansion in their profit margins. This indicates operational efficiency and the ability to convert revenue growth into profits.

- Innovation and Product Development: Companies leading in innovation within their sectors are ideal candidates for growth investing. This can include technological advancements, new products or services, and improvements in existing processes.

- R&D Spending: High spending on research and development (R&D) can be an indicator of a company investing in its future growth.

- Market Size and Potential: Companies operating in markets with significant expansion potential offer substantial growth opportunities. Sectors like technology, biotechnology, and renewable energy are often on the radar of growth investors.

- Competitive Advantage: Companies with high entry barriers in their sector, such as patents, proprietary technology, or a strong brand, have greater potential for sustained growth.

- Product Differentiation: The ability to differentiate products or services from competitors can drive growth.

- Vision and Strategy: The management team must have a clear vision and a well-defined strategy for growth. Their track record of execution and leadership is crucial.

- Adaptability: The ability to adapt to market changes and seize new opportunities is fundamental for long-term success.

Each investment strategy has its own risks and benefits. While value investing strategies may frustrate seasoned investors by keeping a company undervalued indefinitely, growth investing may lead to selecting companies that do not grow as much as anticipated or, worse, whose business model fails, posing financial risks.

Over time and with experience, we can identify the investment spectrum where we feel most comfortable. While growth investing can be volatile, risky, and offer high returns, value investing may be boring, frustrating, or the most obvious investment we have ever made. Therefore, we must find our own space as investors.

Examples of Growth Companies: In its early stages, Amazon focused on aggressive expansion, reinvesting most of its profits into growth. This resulted in massive appreciation of its stock price over the years. On the other hand, Tesla has been an example of a growth company that has transformed the automotive industry with its innovation in electric vehicles and battery technology, resulting in significant growth in its stock value. Lastly, Netflix has shown continuous growth through its global expansion and investment in original content, achieving a dominant position in the streaming market.

These examples illustrate the variables a company must possess to be considered a growth company, but as you may have noticed, investing in these companies during their early stages is incredibly challenging. Success is often confirmed when it becomes obvious to other investors. This situation should alert us to be cautious when attempting to identify the next Amazon, as most companies fail on their path to success.

DIVIDEND INVESTING

Dividend investing is a strategy focused on acquiring shares of companies that regularly pay dividends. This strategy is used to generate a steady stream of passive income, which can be reinvested or used to cover current expenses. Thus, the primary motivation for dividend investing is to obtain stable and regular passive income from received dividends. Companies that pay dividends are often financially stable and well-established, which reduces investment risk.

To develop this strategy, we need to understand several key concepts that are relevant not only when we try to maintain our wealth but also when we aim to grow it through the dividends received. One of the parameters we should examine is the dividend yield. This is the ratio that indicates how much a company pays in dividends annually relative to its stock price. Another important aspect is analyzing a company's dividend payment history, as this information can indicate the company's ability to maintain future dividend payments. Companies with a consistent history of paying and increasing dividends should be our preference.

Advantages of Dividend Investing:

Dividend investing provides a regular source of income that can be especially useful for retirees or those seeking additional income. Additionally, companies known for their dividends tend to be less volatile than those that do not pay dividends.

We should note that dividend investing may not be the most suitable strategy if our primary goal is reinvestment. Besides the taxation that comes with receiving dividends, there might be additional withholdings that reduce our capital and, consequently, our reinvestment. If reinvestment is a crucial part of our strategy, we should consider companies that aggressively repurchase their own shares, known as "cannibal" companies.

Selecting High-Dividend Stocks:

Selecting high-dividend stocks involves identifying companies that not only pay high dividends but also have the capacity to maintain and increase those payments. In addition to analyzing the company's history of dividend increases, it is important to examine the payout ratio. This ratio measures the percentage of a company's earnings that is paid out in dividends. A reasonable payout ratio (typically between 40% and 60%) suggests that the company retains enough capital for reinvestment and growth. However, logically, the lower this ratio, the better the company's ability to not only maintain the dividend but also to make future increases.

On the other hand, without detracting from what has been said, we need to analyze the financial stability of the company through its balance sheet and cash flows. Additionally, we should consider the sector of the company and its cyclicality, as some sectors, such as utilities and consumer staples, are known for stable and consistent dividend payments, even during economic downturns. In contrast, dividends from cyclical companies often exhibit greater variation and may be eliminated during challenging economic periods.

PASSIVE INVESTING

Passive investing is a strategy focused on replicating the returns of a market index rather than attempting to outperform it. This philosophy is based on the premise that markets are generally efficient, and trying to select individual stocks or time the market rarely produces superior returns consistently over the long term. In fact, it has often been shown that beating market performance is frequently an almost impossible task, so passive investing guarantees a decent return with minimal expense and, most importantly, without the need for extensive financial knowledge. To implement passive investing as a primary investment strategy, index funds are commonly used.

An index fund is a type of mutual fund or exchange-traded fund (ETF) designed to track a specific market index, such as the S&P 500, which includes the 500 largest companies in the United States; the Nasdaq 100, which comprises the 100 largest technology companies in the U.S.; or the MSCI World, representing major companies worldwide.

These funds buy all (or a representative sample) of the stocks in the index they are tracking, in the same proportions, thereby achieving the same returns as the index in a simple and efficient manner.

Passive investing, therefore, focuses on the theory of efficient markets. This theory suggests that all available information is already reflected in stock prices, making it difficult to consistently outperform the market. Moreover, index funds offer instant diversification by investing in a broad range of companies within an index, and because they do not require active management, they have lower fees and operational costs compared to actively managed funds.

All of this makes passive investing easy to understand and implement, making it accessible for investors of all experience levels, providing consistent returns that tend to match the overall market. Additionally, passive investors can choose index funds that represent international markets, offering significant geographical diversification.

As previously mentioned, passive investing is an excellent financial tool for those who do not wish to delve deeply into the knowledge needed to invest in individual stocks. These products allow investors to easily and comfortably gain exposure to future stock performance.

However, it is important to remember that investing carries inherent risks, even when done passively and diversely. We must be aware that investment returns come over time, and while waiting for these returns, we need to have the stomach to endure market volatility. This means that, while it is possible to invest and gain exposure to the stock market without extensive economic or financial knowledge, we must develop psychological skills to manage market volatility effectively and avoid making impulsive decisions during the worst market conditions.

Like the great investors

CHAPTER 3:
LEGENDARY INVESTORS AND THEIR STRATEGIES

The world of investing is not just a realm of numbers, markets, and fluctuations; it is also a stage where the brightest and most visionary minds in finance are forged. Investments throughout history have been the battlefield where strategies have competed, philosophies have evolved, and the most captivating personalities have left their indelible mark. These personalities have shaped not only the present of the market but also its future, becoming beacons of inspiration for generations of investors.

In this book, we will delve into the minds and methods of some of the most influential investors of all time, offering a window into their thoughts, decisions, and the principles that have guided their careers.

WARREN BUFFETT: THE ORACLE OF OMAHA

Warren Edward Buffett, born on August 30, 1930, in Omaha, Nebraska, is one of the most iconic figures in the world of investing. Nicknamed "The Oracle of Omaha," Buffett is considered one of the most successful investors in history, known for his prudent approach, incredible ability to identify value opportunities, and long-term focus on wealth creation.

From a young age, Buffett exhibited an unusual interest in business and investing. His father, Howard Buffett, was a stockbroker and a member of the U.S. Congress, and was an early influence in his life. Warren demonstrated a natural talent for numbers and an entrepreneurial spirit from childhood. At the age of six, he bought a pack of six Coca-Cola bottles for 25 cents and sold them for 30 cents, making a small profit. This was just the first step in a career that would eventually make him one of the wealthiest people in the world.

Buffett also showed a penchant for learning from the best. In his teenage years, he read investment books, including the influential "The Intelligent Investor" by Benjamin Graham. This work would become the foundation of his investment philosophy and lead him to enroll at Columbia

Business School, where Graham taught. Under Graham's mentorship, Buffett adopted the value investing approach that would define his career.

Warren Buffett's investment philosophy focuses on value investing, an approach developed by Benjamin Graham. Value investing involves seeking stocks that are undervalued by the market but have a strong likelihood of recovering in the long term. For Buffett, the price of a stock does not always reflect its intrinsic value, and it is precisely in that discrepancy where investment opportunities are found.

Buffett has maintained that patience is one of the most important virtues for an investor. His approach is based on the idea of buying quality companies and holding them for the long term, trusting that their value will be revealed over time. This long-term approach has allowed him to avoid the traps of short-term market fluctuations and take advantage of the sustained growth of his investments.

Furthermore, the long-term approach enables Buffett to benefit from the compound growth of investments. By holding stocks for extended periods, he can take advantage of the power of compounding, where earnings generated from investments are reinvested to generate even more earnings. This approach also reduces the costs associated with frequent buying and selling of stocks, such as brokerage fees and capital gains taxes.

One of Buffett's most famous quotes is: "Our favorite holding period is forever." This reflects his belief in the importance of selecting solid companies with a robust business model, a competent management team, and a durable competitive advantage, and maintaining those investments over the years to maximize returns.

Buffett is also known for avoiding investments he does not fully understand. This is due to his disciplined approach and desire to minimize risk. He prefers to invest in industries and companies with simple and predictable business models, allowing him to better assess their intrinsic value. This approach has kept him away from market fads and bubbles, allowing him to protect and grow his capital consistently.

For Buffett, leadership refers not only to the size of the company or its market share but also to the strength of its business model, its ability to innovate and adapt to changes, and the quality of its management. Leadership is also reflected in the company's ability to generate and maintain high profit margins. Buffett prefers companies that are not only profitable but also have the capacity to maintain and, if possible, increase their profitability over time. This indicates that the company has a solid and sustainable business model that does not depend on temporary or cyclical factors.

Buffett looks for companies with a "durable competitive advantage," allowing them to maintain market leadership for many years. This advantage can come from various factors, such as a strong brand, an efficient distribution network, economies of scale, or intellectual property rights. Coca-Cola, for example, is one of Buffett's most iconic investments precisely because it is a globally recognized brand with a distribution network that gives it a significant edge over its competitors.

Contrary to the popular belief that success in investing relies on constant activity, Buffett argues that inactivity is, in fact, a key component of achieving good results. His approach is simple yet powerful: instead of trying to "time the market" and constantly making transactions, Buffett prefers a more calm and thoughtful approach, carefully selecting his investments and then letting time do its work.

Buffett has said on numerous occasions that "the stock market is a device for transferring money from the impatient to the patient." This statement underscores his belief that sometimes the best investment activity is to do nothing. Staying inactive in the markets during periods of uncertainty or volatility can be more beneficial than trying to guess short-term movements, which is inherently risky and difficult to predict.

On the other hand, one of the most important principles guiding Warren Buffett's investment strategy is avoiding being swayed by the crowd. In the financial world, emotions and market trends can often lead to irrational decisions. Buffett, however, has demonstrated an exceptional ability to stay true to his convictions, even when it means going against the grain.

Buffett has repeatedly mentioned the importance of being "greedy when others are fearful, and fearful when others are greedy." This statement encapsulates his contrarian approach, which involves buying when the market is in panic and stock prices are depressed, and selling when unchecked optimism has inflated prices to unsustainable levels.

History is full of examples where Buffett has defied conventional wisdom. During the tech bubble of the late 1990s, when many investors were captivated by internet companies, Buffett stayed on the sidelines, avoiding investments in a sector he did not fully understand and considered overvalued. Although he was criticized at the time, his prudence proved correct when the bubble burst and many of those companies collapsed.

Market corrections, that is, significant drops in stock prices, are inevitable and part of the normal market cycle. However, while many investors view these corrections with fear, Warren Buffett sees them as opportunities. Instead of panicking and selling when markets fall, Buffett often takes advantage of these situations to buy quality stocks at reduced prices.

Buffett has noted that "opportunities come infrequently. When it rains gold, grab a bucket, not a thimble." This approach underscores his willingness to act decisively during market uncertainty, buying assets he believes are undervalued due to temporary investor panic.

Warren Buffett, known for his ability to simplify complex investment concepts, encapsulates in the following phrase one of the most important distinctions between an average investor and an expert investor: "Diversification is a protection against ignorance. It makes little sense if you know what you're doing." His seemingly controversial statement puts into perspective one of the most commonly accepted strategies in the financial world: diversification.

Generally, diversification is seen as a fundamental tool for managing risk. The logic behind diversification is clear: by spreading investments across a variety of assets and sectors, exposure to the specific risk of any one company or industry is reduced. If one part of the portfolio suffers losses, the idea is that other parts can offset those losses, maintaining the overall balance of the portfolio.

This approach is particularly useful for investors who do not have the time, resources, or experience needed to thoroughly analyze each company in which they invest. For these investors, diversification acts as insurance against ignorance, protecting them from the risks inherent in betting too much on a single asset or sector. It is, in many cases, a way to navigate uncertainty with a certain degree of security.

However, from Warren Buffett's perspective, diversification is not always necessary, especially if an investor has a deep understanding and firm conviction about the investments they make. According to Buffett, an investor who truly understands what they are doing, who has conducted thorough analysis and identified opportunities with clear and sustainable competitive advantages, does not need to protect themselves through broad diversification.

In other words, for Buffett, if you have the ability to accurately identify and assess companies that offer exceptional long-term value, it is better to concentrate your resources on those few exceptional opportunities rather than diluting potential returns through broad diversification. Buffett argues that diversification can, in fact, limit return potential by investing in mediocre companies just to adhere to a diversification principle. For him, a more focused approach, based on rigorous analysis and confidence in investment decisions, can lead to superior long-term returns. The key, of course, lies in "knowing what you're doing": deeply understanding the dynamics of the companies you invest in and being willing to hold those investments through market fluctuations.

Many times, Warren Buffett has expressed how challenging it is to find good investment ideas, and thus understands that when three or four investment ideas that meet the requirements mentioned are found, they are sufficient to invest the entire capital if the confidence in those investments is high.

For investors aiming to apply Buffett's philosophy, the path is clear: instead of simply diversifying, work on improving your ability to analyze and understand the markets and companies you invest in. This does not mean that diversification should be avoided entirely, but it may make less sense if you have developed a level of competence and confidence that allows you to concentrate your investments with assurance.

Finally, and perhaps most importantly, although Buffett is known for his long-term approach and tendency to hold investments for many years, he is not averse to selling if he believes a company no longer meets his investment criteria. The willingness to sell is as important as the decision to buy, and Buffett has demonstrated that he knows when it is the right time to dispose of an investment.

Buffett has sold stocks on several occasions when he has seen that the intrinsic value of a company has been reached or exceeded by the market price, or when the fundamental circumstances that justified the original investment have changed. For example, if a company loses its competitive advantage or if the management team makes decisions that are not consistent with a long-term strategy, Buffett will not hesitate to reduce or eliminate his stake.

This willingness to sell also reflects his disciplined approach to investing. Buffett does not cling to stocks out of loyalty or nostalgia; every investment decision is based on a rational analysis of the facts and future prospects of the company. This objectivity allows him to maximize returns and minimize potential losses, which is key to maintaining positive long-term returns.

Criteria for Selecting Stocks:

Warren Buffett has developed a rigorous set of criteria for selecting stocks, based on his value investing approach. Although Buffett's selection process is highly detailed, some of the key principles include:

- Intrinsic Value and Margin of Safety: Buffett looks for companies whose intrinsic value, that is, the true value based on assets, projected future earnings, and other fundamental factors, is greater than their current market price. The margin of safety is the difference between intrinsic value and market price, and the larger this margin, the more attractive the investment is to Buffett.

- Understandable Businesses: Buffett focuses on companies whose business models he fully understands. He avoids complex or emerging industries where future prospects are uncertain. He prefers simple businesses, such as consumer companies, financial services, and infrastructure companies, where he can more accurately assess risks and opportunities.

- Durable Competitive Advantage: Buffett seeks companies with a sustainable competitive advantage that allows them to maintain market leadership over the long term. This advantage can come from factors like a strong brand, economies of scale, intellectual property rights, or a robust distribution network. Companies like Coca-Cola and American Express are examples of firms that have maintained their leadership position for decades.

- Competent and Ethical Management: Buffett places great emphasis on the quality of a company's management team. He looks for leaders who are competent, transparent, and who manage the business with integrity. Additionally, he prefers teams that reinvest profits wisely for long-term growth, rather than focusing on maximizing short-term results.

- Concentration: For Buffett, excessive diversification is a clear mistake that protects against ignorance. Often, Buffett's portfolio, which contains dozens of stocks, may seem contradictory, but when analyzing the weight of the stocks in his portfolio, we quickly find that in most cases the top five stocks often represent more than 75% of his total portfolio. This concentration is a clear indicator of the confidence he has in certain stocks, and for this, one must have blind faith in the investments made.

- Long-Term Growth Prospects: Buffett invests in companies that, in addition to being strong in the present, have a promising future. He evaluates a company's capacity to grow in the future based on factors such as product or service demand, geographic expansion, and the ability to adapt to market changes. He does not expect exorbitant growth that later does not materialize, but rather anticipates steady and predictable long-term growth that can compound capital over the long term without much upheaval.

Warren Buffett's Investment in See's Candies:

See's Candies is an American company founded in 1921 in Los Angeles, California, by Charles See, his wife Florence, and his mother, Mary See. The company specializes in the manufacture and sale of high-quality chocolates and candies, with a strong reputation based on freshness and the use of top-notch ingredients. Over the years, See's Candies became a household name on the West Coast of the United States, with iconic stores decorated in black and white that evoked a sense of nostalgia and timeless quality.

Warren Buffett, known for his value investing philosophy, has always sought companies with solid fundamentals, sustainable competitive advantages, and a track record of generating consistent cash flow. In 1972, Buffett, along with his partner Charlie Munger, discovered See's Candies, a company that not only fit their value investing approach but also possessed an evident brand power.

Buffett and Munger were introduced to See's Candies through a friend and fellow investor, Bill Ruane, who recommended they examine the company. Although See's Candies was a small company compared to other Berkshire Hathaway investment targets, both were drawn to the strong customer loyalty and profitability of the business.

As Buffett and Munger began analyzing See's Candies, they quickly recognized that the company had a unique competitive advantage. See's had built an iconic brand that resonated deeply with West Coast consumers. This loyalty translated not only into consistent sales but also into the company's ability to maintain premium prices without losing customers, a crucial factor Buffett refers to as "pricing power."

Buffett understood that the value of See's Candies was not just in its physical assets, such as factories and stores, but in its intangible yet powerful brand value. This recognition of brand power was a significant revelation for Buffett, who had always valued tangible assets more. The lesson See's taught him was that a strong brand can be a source of enduring profitability, capable of generating sustained cash flows over time without the need to constantly reinvest large amounts of capital.

Although Buffett and Munger were impressed by See's Candies' strength, the acquisition was not without challenges. The See family, still owning the company, was seeking a sale price that Buffett considered high relative to the company's tangible assets. However, it was Charlie Munger who convinced Buffett that the purchase price was justified due to the strength of the business model and the intangible value of the brand.

Buffett eventually agreed to pay $25 million for See's Candies, a considerable sum at the time for a company with annual earnings of around $4 million. This decision marked a shift in Buffett's investment strategy. Until then, he had favored buying companies at low prices relative to their book value. However, with See's Candies, he learned to appreciate and value the quality of the business above other variables, even if it meant paying a higher price than desired.

The acquisition of See's Candies proved to be a great success for Berkshire Hathaway. From the moment of purchase, See's began generating a significant amount of free cash flow, allowing Buffett and Munger to reinvest those funds into other lucrative opportunities. See's Candies not only remained profitable but also grew steadily in revenue and profit margins without the need for aggressive expansion or reinvestment in its business model.

See's Candies has been a cash-generating machine for Berkshire Hathaway, with returns far exceeding the initial investment. Buffett has repeatedly cited See's as one of the clearest examples of a "wonderful company" with intrinsic value far greater than the tangible book value of its assets. The lesson learned was clear: it is better to pay a fair price for an excellent company than a low price for a mediocre one.

JOEL GREENBLATT: THE LITTLE BOOK THAT BEATS THE MARKET

Joel Greenblatt, born in 1957, is one of the most influential and respected investors in the financial world. While he is primarily known for his book "The Little Book That Still Beats the Market," Greenblatt has had a long and successful career in investing. He graduated from the Wharton School with a degree in economics and later earned an MBA.

After his studies, Greenblatt founded Gotham Capital in 1985, an investment fund that quickly gained notoriety for its impressive returns. Under his leadership, Gotham Capital recorded average annual returns of over 40% for more than a decade, a feat that catapulted him to fame in the investing community. This success was largely due to Greenblatt's discipline, patience, and meticulous approach to stock selection.

Despite his success, Greenblatt always had an interest in teaching and sharing his knowledge with others. He was an adjunct professor at Columbia University, where he taught value investing. His desire to educate and simplify investment concepts led him to write several books, with "The Little Book That Still Beats the Market" being his most popular and accessible work.

In this book, published in 2005, Greenblatt presents an investment strategy he calls "the magic formula." Greenblatt's goal was to explain value investing in such a simple manner that even people who had never heard of investing before could understand it. Joel Greenblatt's investment methodology is relatively straightforward. It involves searching for bargains in the stock market to ensure that the investment's return outweighs the risks, and this book explains how to achieve that.

The book discusses different investment methods associated with various risk profiles. According to Greenblatt, the four ways to use savings are: keeping it under the mattress, leaving it in the bank to earn interest, buying government bonds, or buying company stocks. The author recommends that if we do not want to lose purchasing power due to inflation, we should discard the first two ideas and focus on the latter two, although for Greenblatt, as with other investors, the best way to invest savings will always be through purchasing stocks.

Through a simple formula, Greenblatt ranks publicly traded companies based on their price and profitability, so that the best price-profit combinations appear at the top of the list. Greenblatt suggests that having an automated stock selection system can be beneficial so that investor emotions do not affect their investing approach, as, as discussed, many times in the book, market volatility and trends can sometimes complicate making rational decisions.

Once companies are ranked by price-profitability, a portfolio of 20 stocks should be chosen, which, according to Greenblatt, is sufficient to approach investment with adequate diversification. He also urges that this exercise be done annually. In other words, we should reorder the publicly traded companies and select the top 20 stocks again and purchase them. This short-term rotation (annually) becomes one of the main drawbacks of Joel Greenblatt's strategy, as buying and selling stocks annually can incur significant costs for the investor.

But how do we rank the different publicly traded companies? According to the author, it's through the so-called "magic formula" created by the investor himself. This formula is designed to help investors identify and select stocks that, according to Greenblatt, have a high potential to deliver market-beating returns in the long run. The magic formula is based on two key financial concepts: Return on Capital Employed (ROCE) and Earnings Yield (EY). ROCE measures how efficiently a company uses its capital to generate profits, while EY is the inverse of the price-to-earnings ratio (P/E) and measures how cheap a stock is relative to its earnings.

Greenblatt's magic formula ranks companies based on these two metrics, combining them to identify stocks that have high returns on capital and are undervalued by the market relative to their earnings. The logic behind this strategy is simple: companies that generate high returns on their capital and are undervalued by the market are likely to outperform others over time.

Joel Greenblatt perfectly summarizes his investment approach with the following phrase: "The secret to investing successfully is to find something of value and then pay a lot less for it." This statement, which might seem obvious at first glance, encapsulates one of the most important keys to building wealth consistently over time.

Imagine you are at a silent auction. In the room, several people are evaluating the available items. Some participate fervently, driven by the excitement of the moment and the desire to acquire something exclusive. Others, however, remain silent, carefully observing each item, not just for what it seems worth but for what it truly is. Greenblatt is like that silent observer.

His approach focuses on a thorough search for value. To him, every company in the market is like one of those items at the auction. It doesn't matter what the crowd thinks it's worth; what matters is what it really is. And there lies the essence of his strategy: finding companies that the market has undervalued, buying those stocks at a significantly lower price than their intrinsic value, and then patiently waiting for the market to recognize their true value.

This approach is based on two fundamental pillars: a deep understanding of what constitutes a company's real value and the discipline not to overpay. Greenblatt teaches that the true art of investing is not in following market fads or trying to predict the next big leap but in sticking firmly to the principle of buying value with a significant margin of safety.

"Value" itself is not an abstract concept for Greenblatt; it can be measured and quantified. His "magic formula" is an attempt to systematize this process, combining earnings yield and return on capital to identify those companies that are undervalued. But even with a formula, successful investing requires more: the patience and discipline to wait for the market to correct its valuation errors.

The magic of this strategy is its simplicity. In a world where investors are often tempted by complexities and promises of quick wealth, Greenblatt reminds us that the best investments are those that are easily understood and bought at a significant discount to their true value. Thus, success in investing doesn't come from complexity but from clarity in valuing and executing the purchase.

For investors who follow this path, the reward is twofold: not only do they achieve financial returns, but they also gain the peace of mind of knowing they have made a sensible investment based on solid fundamentals. And, just like at that silent auction, it is those who remain calm, calculating, and evaluating who end up with the best deals.

As we see, many of the concepts that Joel Greenblatt applies to investing are also used by Warren Buffett. As we will see, value investors rely on the same basic principles of investing. The only difference lies in how these principles are applied, as well as the level of diversification used or the companies selected.

In addition to the above, Greenblatt emphasizes the importance of understanding the stocks you buy. In another famous quote, Joel Greenblatt warns of the dangers of investing when guided by ignorance: "Picking individual stocks without any idea of what you're looking for is like walking through a dynamite factory with a lit match. You might survive, but you're still an idiot." Investing in the stock market may seem exciting and full of opportunities, but it can also be incredibly risky if approached without proper preparation. Joel Greenblatt, in his characteristically blunt and direct style, compares this lack of preparation to an extremely dangerous situation: walking through a dynamite factory with a lit match. The image is powerful and clear: the danger lies not only in the action but in the recklessness of doing it without a clear guide or defined purpose.

For Greenblatt, the act of picking individual stocks without a strategy is extremely reckless. Many investors enter the market hoping for great returns but without a clear understanding of what they are looking for or what factors should guide their selection. They follow fleeting trends, are swayed by rumors, or buy stocks because "everyone else is doing it." However, this approach is not only ineffective but also extremely dangerous.

Stock selection is not a game of chance, nor an activity where luck can replace judgment. Greenblatt insists that investors must have a clear idea of what they are seeking: a set of criteria to evaluate investment opportunities. This might include solid fundamental analysis, an understanding of a company's intrinsic value, and a careful assessment of the associated risks. Only with this knowledge and preparation can an investor make informed decisions and avoid the pitfalls that await those who operate without a plan.

Thus, Greenblatt warns us that survival in the stock market should not depend on chance or luck. It should be based on a methodical and disciplined approach, where each investment decision is backed by careful analysis and a clear understanding of what is being sought. Only in this way can one successfully navigate the complex and often volatile world of investing, minimizing risks and maximizing the chances of success.

The Components of the Magic Formula

Joel Greenblatt's Magic Formula is based on two key financial metrics: Return on Capital Employed (ROCE) and Earnings Yield. These metrics are chosen for their ability to identify companies that are not only profitable but also undervalued by the market.

- Return on Capital Employed (ROCE): This metric measure how efficiently a company uses its capital to generate profits. It indicates whether the company is using its resources to generate benefits and to what extent. Greenblatt selects ROCE because he believes that companies generating high returns on their capital are better positioned to deliver superior returns in the long run. ROCE is calculated as operating income divided by the sum of working capital and net fixed assets. This approach helps identify companies that are generating solid returns relative to the capital invested in their operations.

- Earnings Yield: This is the inverse of the price-to-earnings (P/E) ratio and is used to measure how cheap a stock is relative to its earnings. Greenblatt prefers earnings yield because it is a direct way to assess whether a stock is undervalued. It is calculated by dividing earnings before interest and taxes (EBIT) by enterprise value, which includes both the market value of the company and its net debt. A high earnings yield indicates that the company is generating significant income relative to its market price, suggesting it may be undervalued.

The Magic Formula ranks companies based on these two metrics. First, the ROCE and earnings yield of each company in a given universe of stocks (e.g., companies listed on U.S. stock markets) are calculated. Then, each company is ranked separately based on these two metrics.

After ranking companies according to these two metrics, the rankings are summed to obtain a composite ranking. The companies with the lowest composite rankings (i.e., those that rank high in terms of ROCE and earnings yield) are selected for investment. These companies are considered the most attractive according to the Magic Formula because they are profitable and undervalued, making them ideal candidates for superior returns.

On the other hand, what has set Joel Greenblatt apart in his investing approach is his focus on "special situations" that frequently occur in the stock market. In his other book, "You Can Be a Stock Market Genius," Greenblatt delves into a more advanced topic: special situations in investing. This book is a guide to identifying and capitalizing on investment opportunities that, although less known and unconventional, can yield extraordinary returns.

Special situations refer to unique circumstances within companies that can create highly profitable investment opportunities. These situations include corporate events such as mergers and acquisitions, spin-offs, restructurings, bankruptcies, recapitalizations, and secondary public offerings. Greenblatt argues that due to the complexity and lack of attention from traditional investors towards these events, significant bargains can be found in the market.

Greenblatt's book is filled with practical strategies for identifying and evaluating these special situations. He teaches readers how to read between the lines in corporate announcements and financial reports, looking for signals that indicate hidden investment potential. Some of the strategies Greenblatt discusses in his book include:

- Spin-offs: A spin-off occurs when a parent company decides to separate one of its divisions or business units into a new independent entity. Shareholders of the parent company usually receive shares of the new company proportionally. Spin-offs are generally done to unlock hidden value in a specific division that might be undervalued or overlooked within the parent company. The new entity can focus more effectively on its core business without the burden of the parent company. Therefore, spin-offs can be a goldmine for astute investors. Often, shares of the new company can be quickly sold off by institutional investors who do not wish to hold them, which may create downward pressure on the price during the first days or weeks of trading. This phenomenon can offer the opportunity to buy shares at an attractive price before the market recognizes the true value of the new entity.

- Mergers and Acquisitions: A merger or acquisition occurs when a company buys or merges with another. These events can be friendly or hostile and may involve cash transactions, stock transactions, or a combination of both. In a merger or acquisition, the acquiring company will pay a premium over the current stock price of the target company. This creates expectations about the successful completion of the deal and the potential revaluation of the shares. Investors can exploit the price differences between the current market value and the offer price in mergers and acquisitions. However, these events carry significant risks, such as the possibility that the deal may not go through, which could lead to a drop in the target company's stock price.

- Restructurings: A restructuring involves significant changes to a company's financial or operational structure. This may include asset sales, debt reduction, layoffs, or even a business refocus. Restructurings are generally done in response to financial problems or to optimize the company's efficiency. The goal is to make the company more profitable or prepare it for eventual growth or sale. Restructurings can turn struggling companies into success stories, offering investors the opportunity to benefit from the recovery. Investing in a company undergoing a restructuring can be risky, but if the restructuring is successful, the potential return can be significant, although this type of investment should be made only by more advanced investors.

- Recapitalizations: A recapitalization is a process in which a company changes its capital structure, typically by issuing debt to repurchase shares, or issuing new shares to reduce debt. Recapitalizations are usually done to optimize the company's capital structure, improve profitability, or fend off an unwanted acquisition. They can involve an increase in the company's debt, which raises financial risk, but it can also enhance the return on equity. Investors can benefit from recapitalizations by identifying companies that, despite taking on more debt, could generate superior returns due to a more efficient capital structure. Like restructurings, these are investments with potential risk.

- Bankruptcies and Reorganizations: Bankruptcy occurs when a company cannot meet its financial obligations and seeks protection under bankruptcy laws. A reorganization is an attempt to restructure the company's operations and debts to continue operating. In bankruptcy, shareholders often lose most or all of their investment. However, creditors may receive new securities as part of the reorganization, and sometimes shareholders receive shares in the reorganized company. Investing in bankrupt or reorganizing companies can be extremely risky but may offer significant opportunities if the company manages to recover and emerge stronger and more profitable. Investors must be very cautious and have a deep understanding of the company's financial situation before investing in such situations.

- Secondary Public Offerings: A secondary public offering is the sale of additional shares to the public after an initial public offering (IPO). These shares can be new or sold by existing shareholders. Companies conduct secondary offerings to raise additional capital, which may dilute the value of existing shares but can also strengthen the company's financial position. Secondary offerings can create buying opportunities if prices fall due to dilution, but investors should carefully evaluate the purpose of the offering and its potential impact on the company before investing.

- Divestitures: A divestiture occurs when a company sells a portion of its assets or an entire division to focus on its core business or to raise funds. Divestitures allow companies to streamline their operations and focus on more profitable areas, often unlocking hidden value in the sold assets. Investors can benefit from divestitures by buying shares of the selling company if the sale strengthens its balance sheet or acquiring shares of the buying company if the acquired assets are considered valuable.

These are some of the special situations detailed in Greenblatt's book, which represent a completely different approach to investing. By leveraging these circumstances, which pose greater complexity for novice investors, Greenblatt capitalized on opportunities where others did not see or know how to exploit value. By seeking value where others do not or cannot see it, investors can take advantage of market inefficiencies and achieve significant short-term returns. These special situations can always be a good complement to other, more long-term investments, but the difficulty and risk associated with this type of investing should always be considered.

MICHAEL BURRY: THE VISIONARY OF THE GREAT RECESSION

Michael Burry was born on June 19, 1971, in San Jose, California. From a young age, Burry demonstrated a penchant for analysis and research, which would later become the foundation of his unique approach in the world of finance. Despite losing an eye to cancer as a child and having to use a glass eye, Burry did not let this challenge affect his determination. His interest in medicine led him to study at the University of California, where he earned a degree in economics and pre-medicine. He then attended the Vanderbilt University School of Medicine and completed his neurology residency at Stanford University.

However, while still in medical school, Burry began to develop a growing interest in the financial market. This interest soon turned into a passion that led him to spend more time studying the stock market than attending his medical studies. Using his blog, Burry began sharing detailed financial analyses focused on stock selection based on thorough fundamental analysis. This blog attracted the attention of many on Wall Street, who recognized Burry's analytical talent and urged him to pursue a career in finance.

Michael Burry's investment strategy is based on a deep and thorough analysis of financial data, a skill he likely developed during his medical training, where attention to detail is crucial, as well as his autism spectrum disorder, which always made socializing difficult and made him feel different from others.

Burry does not follow market fads or trends. Instead, he focuses on the fundamentals of the companies he invests in, seeking out those that are undervalued or misunderstood by the market and investing in them, expecting significant appreciation.

One of the main features of his strategy is his inclination towards "value investing," an approach popularized by Benjamin Graham and Warren Buffett. However, Burry took this approach a step further, using his deep analysis to identify opportunities that others overlooked, specializing in what are known as "special situations." These are companies facing temporary problems that have caused a sharp decline in their stock prices, but have a solid underlying base and high recovery potential.

In recent years, Burry has altered his investment style. Unlike other value investors who prefer to hold their stocks for long periods, Burry now holds them for only a few months. This new, more chaotic and disorganized investment style makes it more challenging to follow Burry's reasoning and even more so to try to mimic his investment style.

Burry is also known for his ability to identify asset bubbles and position himself to benefit from their eventual collapse. Instead of simply following stock price signals, Burry examines broader financial and economic data, analyzing how these factors could affect the long-term value of investments. His approach is that of a detective, scrutinizing every detail to build a complete picture that allows him to anticipate significant market movements.

However, Burry became globally known as an investor thanks to the 2008 financial crisis. The name Michael Burry is synonymous with foresight and audacity in the financial world, but his rise to fame was neither simple nor free of challenges. His legacy was built on sharp vision, deep analytical capability, and a willingness to question conventional wisdom at a time when the market seemed irrefutably optimistic. To understand how Burry became a key figure in modern financial history, it is crucial to analyze the events that led him to foresee the 2008 financial crisis and the decisions he made to capitalize on his prediction.

In the early 2000s, the United States experienced an unprecedented real estate boom. Housing prices were steadily rising, fueled by a mortgage lending policy that seemed to benefit both borrowers and lenders. Banks and other financial institutions began issuing mortgages to individuals with low credit ratings, known as "subprime," under the assumption that the real estate market would continue to rise and that even if borrowers defaulted, rising home prices would cover the losses.

The enthusiasm for the real estate market was so great that these "subprime" mortgages were packaged into mortgage-backed securities (MBS), which were sold to investors as safe and profitable assets. The prevailing logic was that, due to the diversification of these packages, the risk of default was diluted, making them attractive to investment funds, banks, and other actors in the global financial market.

However, Michael Burry, a doctor turned investor who managed his own hedge fund, Scion Capital, was not swayed by the widespread optimism. Instead of relying on Wall Street's assurances, Burry focused on conducting a thorough analysis of the "subprime" mortgages and the MBS that contained them. What he discovered was unsettling: many of these loans had been made to individuals who, under normal circumstances, would never have qualified for credit, and they were structured in such a way that they were extremely vulnerable to any changes in market conditions.

Burry was not a traditional economist, nor did he come from a major investment firm; his competitive edge lay in his ability to study data meticulously without prejudice or preconceived notions. In his analysis, Burry examined the default rates of "subprime" mortgages, the terms of the loans, and the internal structure of the MBS. He soon realized that the default rates were much higher than publicly reported and that adjustable-rate loans, which allowed for low payments initially but increased over time, would be unsustainable for borrowers when rates rose or home prices stabilized or fell.

Burry also identified that many borrowers were too highly leveraged, meaning they had taken on debts far beyond what they could manage with their income. This meant that any small disturbance in the market, such as an increase in interest rates or a slowdown in the rise of home prices, could lead to a massive increase in default rates, which would, in turn, cause the MBS linked to these mortgages to collapse.

Despite clear signs of an imminent collapse, most of Wall Street and other key players in the financial market continued to act as if the real estate boom would never end. It was in this context that Burry made a bold decision that would change his life and the history of finance.

In 2005, armed with his conviction that the real estate market was destined to collapse, Burry began looking for a way to profit from what he saw as an inevitable disaster. He discovered that he could bet against the MBS by buying credit default swaps (CDS), a type of insurance that would pay out if the mortgage-backed securities failed. The idea was simple in theory but risky in practice: Burry was betting that the MBS, considered by many to be solid assets, would lose value when the underlying mortgages began to default.

This strategy was met with skepticism and disbelief by many on Wall Street. After all, who would bet against a market that seemed to be rising endlessly? But Burry was undeterred. Despite pressure from investors in his own fund who doubted his strategy, Burry pressed on, securing billions of dollars in CDS against the MBS. For a time, it seemed his detractors were right: the real estate market continued to grow, and the CDS payments were draining resources from Scion Capital, leading some investors to withdraw.

However, Burry was convinced of his analysis. He knew that the economic fundamentals could not support the bubble forming in the real estate market. For him, it was only a matter of time before reality set in and the market collapsed.

In 2007, the warning signs became impossible to ignore. Default rates on "subprime" mortgages began to rise dramatically. Financial institutions that had accumulated large amounts of MBS began to feel the pressure, and the real estate market, which had until then been seen as invulnerable, started to wobble. When "subprime" borrowers could no longer keep up with their mortgage payments and home prices stopped rising, the system built on these mortgages collapsed.

The domino effect was swift and devastating. The MBS, which had been sold as safe assets, plummeted in value, and the financial institutions holding them suffered massive losses. What began as a crisis in the real estate sector quickly became a global financial crisis, affecting banks, investment funds, and economies around the world.

For Michael Burry, however, this collapse validated his analysis and strategy. While many on Wall Street lost fortunes, Scion Capital posted spectacular returns, exceeding 400% during this period. Burry's bet was not only financially lucrative but also cemented him as one of the sharpest and most foresighted minds in modern investing, and his story was immortalized in the book and film "The Big Short," which dramatize the events leading up to the financial crisis and highlight Burry's crucial role in anticipating the collapse.

After the 2008 financial crisis, Michael Burry closed Scion Capital to take a break and focus on his personal life. However, his passion for investing led him back to the market with a new approach. He founded Scion Asset Management, where he continued to apply his investment style based on deep analysis and identifying opportunities that others might overlook.

In recent years, Burry has continued to surprise the markets with his bold and unconventional moves. He has invested in sectors such as technology, water, and precious metals, and has made warnings about potential bubbles in various market segments, including the U.S. stock market and cryptocurrencies.

A distinctive aspect of his current approach is his concern with macroeconomic issues and potential future crises. Burry has expressed concern about the growing global debt and the long-term effects of expansive monetary policies, such as massive money printing and ultra-low interest rates. He believes that these policies could be setting the stage for an even greater economic crisis than the one in 2008.

Despite his pessimistic outlook in some areas, Burry remains a strong advocate of value investing and deep analysis. His ability to identify imbalances and hidden opportunities continues to guide his investment decisions, maintaining him as one of the most respected and feared minds in the financial world.

Like other investors we have seen and will see later in this book, Michael Burry relies on value fundamentals. "All my stock selection is based 100% on the concept of margin of safety." In this statement, Burry emphasizes the importance of basing stock purchases on a fundamental value investing concept like the margin of safety, which is defined, as we have seen, as the difference between the market price of an asset and its intrinsic or real value.

Burry can be considered one of the foremost examples of what is known as a contrarian investor. This concept, which we have not yet covered, also accurately represents the typical attitude of value investors. These investors go against the prevailing market sentiment. When the market is buying, the contrarian sells, and vice versa. Contrarian investors look for opportunities to buy in a bearish market and to sell in a bullish market.

Burry perfectly summarizes this sentiment with the following phrase: "Don't worry about missing out on a rally. Worry about losing your money." This statement, which encapsulates a fundamental truth about investing, is a reminder that focus and discipline are more important than chasing quick and fleeting gains.

A market rally is a period when asset prices rise rapidly, generating excitement among investors. During these times, it is common for the fear of missing out ("FOMO") to take hold of many. Collective euphoria, fueled by stories of sudden gains, can cloud judgment and lead to hasty decisions. Investors who were previously cautious and methodical may be swept up in the excitement, fearing they will be left behind while others achieve spectacular returns. However, Burry warns against this mindset. For him, the priority should always be to protect capital, not to chase market trends.

Losing money is more than just a decrease in the bank account; it is a loss of future opportunities. Every dollar lost is a dollar that cannot be used to take advantage of new investment opportunities. This is the core of Burry's philosophy: the primary goal of any investor should be to protect their capital. Rallies, no matter how attractive they seem, may be inflated by bubbles of irrationality and excessive optimism. Participating in them without a clear strategy can lead to devastating losses when the market inevitably corrects.

As we have seen, the most notable example of Burry resisting the temptation of a rally occurred in the years leading up to the 2008 crisis. While housing prices soared and the real estate market seemed to offer endless gains, Burry maintained his focus on fundamentals.

For Burry, rallies are often symptoms of a market that has lost touch with reality. Logic is replaced by emotion, and fundamental valuations give way to rampant speculation, which anticipates significant losses for investors participating in the excitement.

Finally, it is important to highlight Michael Burry's constant adaptation to new investment circumstances. Unlike other, more traditional investors, Burry prefers to adapt to new forms of investing while still keeping value investing principles in mind. For example, something that surprised and was discussed in several interviews is his use of technical analysis in his investments. While many of his contemporaries, like Warren Buffett, tend to ignore technical analysis, Burry uses it to determine the best time to enter an investment. This approach is based on the idea that, although a stock may be undervalued from a fundamental perspective, the market may take a long time to recognize its true value. During this period, the stock could remain stagnant for a long time or even decrease in value, which could negatively impact the investment's performance.

Burry understands that the market is not always efficient and that emotions and short-term trends can significantly influence stock prices. Technical analysis allows him to read these market signals and make informed decisions about when is the right time to buy or sell a stock. This approach not only optimizes the timing of entry but also helps mitigate the risk of holding an undervalued investment for an extended period without seeing a significant return.

As we see, most value investors tend to ignore charts and short-term market trends, trusting that eventually, the intrinsic value of a stock will be reflected in its market price. However, Burry prefers to use technical analysis to determine the best time to buy a stock.

Burry has expressed on several occasions that investing too early in an undervalued stock can be as detrimental as investing in an overvalued one. Excessive anticipation of a market change can lead to capital being stuck in an unproductive investment for years, which not only affects the overall performance of the portfolio but also limits the investor's ability to take advantage of other opportunities that may arise.

This idea is an evolution he has applied to his new investment style. It is important to remember that during the 2008 crisis, when he bet against subprime mortgages, Burry had to watch his investment diminish day by day for almost two years. Added to this was the criticism he had to endure from other investors and his own investors, as well as the widespread pressure from the Wall Street environment. Finally, as we have discussed, Burry achieved unprecedented investment success, but that period marked him so deeply that he approached investing from a different perspective, using technical analysis to identify potential inflection points in the market. These may include price patterns, trading volumes, and other technical signals suggesting that the market is beginning to recognize a stock's underlying value.

PETER LYNCH: INVESTING IN WHAT YOU KNOW

Peter Lynch, one of the most successful and respected investors of all time, was born on January 19, 1944, in Newton, Massachusetts. His childhood was marked by tragedy when he lost his father at a young age, which forced his mother to assume the financial responsibility of the family. This experience instilled in Lynch a strong sense of responsibility and an early understanding of the value of money.

Lynch attended Boston College, where he studied finance and graduated in 1965. During his college years, he developed an increasing interest in the stock market, influenced by his work as a caddie at a local golf club. In this environment, he had the opportunity to overhear conversations among successful entrepreneurs and investors, which sparked his fascination with the world of finance.

After graduating, Lynch continued his education at the Wharton School of the University of Pennsylvania, where he earned an MBA. Shortly thereafter, in 1969, he joined Fidelity Investments as an analyst. His sharp business sense and ability to identify investment opportunities quickly led to promotions, and by 1977, he was named manager of the Magellan Fund, which at that time had a relatively modest asset value of $18 million.

There is no denying that Peter Lynch's career at Fidelity Magellan is legendary. During the 13 years he managed the fund, he achieved an average annual return of 29.2%, consistently outperforming the market and growing the fund's assets to over $14 billion by 1990, when he retired. This achievement is even more impressive considering that Lynch managed a fund with a portfolio that peaked at 1,400 stocks.

Peter Lynch, one of the most iconic figures in the investment world, developed a philosophy that democratized the investing process, moving it away from complex financial models and closer to everyday knowledge. The essence of his approach, encapsulated in the phrase "Invest in what you know," reflected his belief that investment opportunities are within everyone's reach, even those without a deep technical understanding of financial markets.

Lynch believed that individual investors, unlike Wall Street analysts, have a unique advantage: their daily experiences and ability to observe their surroundings. For him, a visit to the supermarket, a walk through the mall, or a casual conversation at work could reveal early signs of products or services gaining popularity. These observations, if recognized and acted upon in time, could translate into investment opportunities before large investment firms detected them.

For example, if an investor notices that a local store is always full of customers or that a specific product is consistently sold out on shelves, they might investigate further into the company behind that success. Lynch encouraged investors to ask basic questions: How solid is the company? Is it financially stable? Is it well managed? Is it expanding? This type of analysis, based on real-world observations, could provide a solid foundation for investment decisions.

Moreover, Lynch firmly believed in the importance of personal research and the need for investors to feel comfortable and familiar with the companies they invest in. This not only increased the likelihood of success but also provided the investor with greater peace of mind during periods of market volatility. By understanding the business and its potential, investors were less prone to panic and sell during a temporary market downturn.

One of the most notable aspects of Lynch's philosophy is his focus on "common sense." He rejected the idea that only experts with access to insider data or advanced mathematical models could succeed in the market. Instead, he encouraged investors to trust their instincts and personal knowledge. For Lynch, the key to success was not having access to privileged information or being a financial genius, but paying attention to the environment, doing the research on companies, and, most importantly, investing in companies they understood and believed in.

This approach, while simple in theory, required discipline and patience. Lynch advised investors not to be swayed by market fads or short-term speculative trends. Instead of seeking quick gains, he advocated for long-term investment in solid companies whose success stories were evident to those who paid attention. This meant holding stocks for years, allowing the growth of the business and accumulation of value to be reflected in the stock price over time.

As he himself warned: "You can lose money in the short term, but you need the long term to make money." This phrase encapsulates one of the most important lessons in the world of investing: patience and a long-term perspective are essential for financial success.

In the context of investing, the short term is filled with uncertainties and volatility. The stock market can experience significant fluctuations due to a variety of factors, from unexpected economic news to changes in government policies, global events, or even market psychology. These fluctuations can cause stock prices to rise or fall abruptly, often without an underlying fundamental reason. This means that, in the short term, investors may see the value of their investments decline, which can lead to worry, fear, or even panic.

Peter Lynch understood that these temporary declines, while disconcerting, are a natural part of investing. For him, short-term losses should not deter investors from staying committed to their decisions. On the contrary, Lynch maintained that the key to achieving substantial gains in the market lies in maintaining a long-term perspective.

Peter Lynch's philosophy is embodied in his distinctive approach known as "growth investing." This approach, which differs notably from the "value investing" popularized by giants like Benjamin Graham and Warren Buffett, focuses not on finding undervalued stocks relative to their intrinsic value, but on identifying companies that are in the midst of expansion and show strong growth potential.

For Lynch, "growth investing" involves seeking companies that are not only experiencing an increase in revenues, but also achieving a sustained rise in earnings. These companies are often in the early or intermediate stages of their life cycle, meaning they have a long way to go before reaching their full potential. Frequently, these companies operate in emerging sectors or markets where the demand for products or services is growing rapidly, or in industries where innovation and disruption are creating new opportunities.

Lynch believed that these types of companies had the potential to deliver returns significantly higher than the broader market. His approach focused on identifying these opportunities before the rest of the market did, allowing him to enter positions at relatively low prices and benefit from price increases as more investors recognized the value of these growing companies.

However, Peter Lynch also warned about the dangers of basing investment decisions solely on personal liking for a product or store. His phrase, "Just because you like a product or store doesn't mean it's a good reason to invest in its stock. Investments are businesses, and businesses aren't managed by appearances" reflects a key lesson in his investment philosophy:

superficial appeal of a product or brand does not guarantee the financial success of the company behind it.

Lynch understood that investors, especially those with little experience, might be tempted to buy stock in a company simply because they liked what it sold. It's easy to fall into this trap. For example, a store that is always full of customers or a product that goes viral might give the impression of being a safe and profitable investment. However, Lynch insisted that such superficial appeal could be an initial clue, but not sufficient to justify an investment.

This style of investing required a combination of analysis and observation. Lynch did not only focus on financial statements and numbers showing a company's growth, but also paid close attention to qualitative factors like company management, market position, and the ability to innovate. He was interested in companies with clear business models, differentiated products or services, and a competitive edge that allowed them to maintain and expand their market share over time.

However, Lynch did not get carried away by enthusiasm alone. Before investing, he conducted a detailed analysis of the companies, focusing on factors such as the price-to-earnings (P/E) ratio, earnings growth, company debt, industry structure, and the quality of the management team. This approach helped him identify not only companies with a solid track record of growth, but also those capable of sustaining that growth in the future.

Once Peter Lynch identified a potential investment target, his process did not end there. Lynch began his analysis by thoroughly reviewing the company's financial statements. For him, these documents were not just numbers, but a story revealing the company's financial health, profitability, and future growth potential. He carefully examined revenues, profit margins, cash flow, and debt, among other key aspects.

In addition to the numbers, Lynch sought to gain a qualitative perspective on the company. Whenever possible, he aimed to speak directly with management. For Lynch, the leadership of a company was crucial; he believed that good management could make the difference between a company that merely survives and one that thrives. He wanted to understand the executives' vision, long-term strategy, and how they planned to address market challenges. Through these conversations, Lynch assessed the confidence, competence, and passion of business leaders, giving him a better idea of whether they were well-positioned to guide the company towards sustained growth.

Another essential part of his analysis was evaluating the industry in which the company operated. Lynch understood that even a well-managed company could face difficulties if it operated in a declining or highly competitive sector without a distinguishing advantage. Therefore, he spent time studying market trends, competition, and economic forces that could impact the company. This allowed him not only to understand the company's current position, but also to anticipate how it might evolve in the future and what challenges or opportunities it might face.

Additionally, as mentioned, a key tool in Lynch's analytical arsenal was the price-to-earnings (P/E) ratio. However, he did not rely on the P/E ratio in isolation. Lynch was a strong proponent of the "PEG ratio," which is the result of dividing a company's P/E ratio by its earnings growth rate. This ratio provided him with a more comprehensive measure of whether a company was undervalued in relation to its growth potential. A low PEG ratio suggested that the company might be undervalued by the market, making it an attractive investment opportunity. For Lynch, this approach allowed him to identify stocks that were not only cheap in terms of P/E but also had significant growth prospects, potentially leading to substantial appreciation in their stock prices.

Lynch believed that finding companies with a favorable PEG ratio was an effective way to balance risk and reward. By investing in companies that were not only financially healthy but also undervalued in terms of future growth, Lynch maximized his potential for high returns while mitigating the risk of investing in overvalued companies.

In his famous book "One up on Wall Street," Lynch highlights what he considers to be one of the absolute truths in the investment world, based on his years as an investor: "the five-stock rule." Peter Lynch states, "If you pick stocks in five different growth companies, you'll find that three will do as expected, one will get into serious trouble, and the fifth will do better than you could have imagined and will surprise you with an exceptional return."

"Since it's impossible to predict which companies will do better than expected and which will do worse, the recommendation is that your portfolio should have no fewer than five stocks," Lynch explains in his renowned book.

Unlike other successful investors like Warren Buffett, Lynch believed in diversification, accumulating up to 1,400 stocks in his portfolio. While this was due to the large capital he managed at the time, which made it challenging to concentrate his portfolio more, Peter Lynch always advocated for sufficient diversification, meaning between 20 and 30 stocks, to minimize risk while also having the chance to invest in "10 baggers."

This term popularized by Lynch refers to an investment whose value increases tenfold. For example, if you invest $1,000 in a stock and its price rises to a total value of $10,000, that stock has become a "10 bagger." The term originates from baseball, where "bagger" refers to the bases reached by the batter. In the context of investments, it is used to describe stocks that have experienced exceptional growth, multiplying their value several times.

For Peter Lynch, the characteristics a company needed to become a "10 bagger" were: companies experiencing accelerated growth in revenues and earnings, operating in sectors or industries in an expansion phase, having some form of competitive advantage, and possessing competent management teams with a history of making sound strategic decisions.

Lynch's investment in The Limited is one of the most emblematic examples of his strategy for identifying "10 baggers." This case not only highlights Lynch's skill in finding exceptional market opportunities, but also his meticulous approach to fundamental analysis and his ability to foresee long-term growth potential.

The Limited was founded in 1963 by Leslie Wexner in Columbus, Ohio. The store started as a small clothing establishment offering affordable fashion for young women. What made The Limited unique was its focus on a specific market niche: modern and accessible clothing for young women who wanted to keep up with trends without spending a fortune. This business strategy allowed it to grow rapidly and capture the attention of consumers at a time when youth fashion was booming.

While managing the Fidelity Magellan Fund, Peter Lynch was constantly on the lookout for companies with scalable business models and significant expansion potential. The Limited caught his attention due to its store concept, which was not only aligned with contemporary trends but also had a replicable model in different markets.

Lynch observed that the company had a clearly defined and growing target audience. Young women were a demographic group increasing their purchasing power and seeking affordable fashion. On the other hand, The Limited was strategically opening new stores in shopping malls and urban areas with high concentrations of young people. This geographic expansion allowed the company to quickly increase its sales and reach a larger customer base. Additionally, Lynch noted that The Limited managed its inventory exceptionally well, minimizing the risk of losses and maximizing product turnover. This was crucial in the fashion industry, where trends change rapidly. Finally, Wexner, the founder of The Limited, not only had a clear vision for the company but was also willing to adapt to changing market needs. This ability to innovate and adjust to trends was fundamental to the company's continued success.

As The Limited continued to expand, the company's revenues and earnings grew at a spectacular rate. The company capitalized on the growth trend in shopping malls during the 1970s and 1980s, establishing its presence nationwide. Additionally, Wexner diversified the business by launching new brands and product lines under The Limited umbrella, such as Victoria's Secret, which would become an iconic global brand.

The success of The Limited's expansion and diversification strategy was reflected in its stock price. During the period Lynch held the investment, The Limited's stock multiplied several times, becoming a true "10 bagger" in the Fidelity Magellan Fund's portfolio. This growth was driven by the constant increase in sales, improved profit margins, and international expansion.

This is just one example of the dozens of stocks that Peter Lynch held in his portfolio, which only increased in value during his management years. Undoubtedly, Lynch became one of the most renowned investors in history. His investment talks capture the public's attention, as he has a remarkable ability to convey the complex and difficult knowledge that the world of investing holds for those who pursue financial and economic success with effort and tenacity.

RAY DALIO: PRINCIPLES AND BRIDGEWATER APPROACH

Ray Dalio, founder of Bridgewater Associates, one of the largest and most successful hedge funds in the world, is a prominent name in the global investment arena. His story begins in Queens, New York, where he was born on August 8, 1949. Raised in a middle-class family, at the age of 12, and like Peter Lynch, he began working as a caddie at a golf course, where he would listen to players talk about investments. Fascinated by these conversations, he decided to invest his first savings in Northeast Airlines stock, a modest experiment that tripled his investment. This early experience sparked a passion for financial markets that would guide the rest of his life.

Dalio graduated in finance from Long Island University and later earned an MBA from Harvard Business School. After briefly working at several financial firms, he founded Bridgewater Associates in 1975 in his two-bedroom apartment in Manhattan. What began as a small financial advisory firm eventually grew into one of the most influential hedge funds in the world, known for its principle-based approach and its ability to successfully navigate various economic cycles.

Although Ray Dalio's path in the investment world resembled that of the phoenix, the mythical bird that rises from its own ashes, more than that of a successful investor like Warren Buffett, he faced significant challenges before establishing what would become the largest hedge fund in the world. Dalio encountered a series of setbacks, including losing investors, clients, and a considerable amount of money due to a failed prediction. For Dalio, this experience proved to be one of the most difficult but also one of the most valuable in his life.

In the 1980s, Dalio was on the brink of bankruptcy with his hedge fund, Bridgewater Associates. At a critical moment, he had to ask his father for a $4,000 loan to support his family. This extremely tough experience, as the investor would later share, was a crucial turning point for him.

Facing ruin taught Ray Dalio a vital lesson: the importance of accepting and learning from mistakes, as well as taking full responsibility for decisions. Instead of holding onto the belief that he was always right, Dalio began to constantly question himself: "How can I be sure I'm right?" These painful experiences, although hard to confront, became valuable lessons that offered him an opportunity to improve and refine his approach moving forward.

Ray Dalio also realized that the best way to assess risks was to surround himself with a team with divergent perspectives. The experience of working with people who did not always agree with him taught him to keep an open mind, testing his ideas and allowing him to compare different viewpoints. This strategy is supported by numerous studies suggesting that "diversity of thought" can provide a significant competitive advantage for companies.

After facing failure, Dalio completely transformed his approach to management. Today, he is one of the wealthiest individuals in the world. Learning from his mistakes, the founder of Bridgewater Associates has accumulated a net worth of $22 billion, according to Forbes magazine.

Ray Dalio's approach to investing is based on a deep understanding of global macroeconomics. Throughout his career, Dalio has developed a methodology that views the behavior of the economy as an interconnected system of markets and policies, what he calls the "economic machine." This macroeconomic approach has allowed Bridgewater to anticipate and adapt to major changes in the global economic landscape.

Dalio believes that financial markets are driven by the dynamics of supply and demand, and that economic cycles are inevitable. For him, the key to success in investing is understanding these cycles and how they interact with monetary and fiscal policies. Through his analysis, Dalio identifies imbalances in the economy that can lead to investment opportunities. This approach allowed him to foresee events like the 2008 financial crisis, during which Bridgewater earned significant profits while other funds suffered losses.

For Ray Dalio, having a global perspective on macroeconomics provides an excellent framework for working. So, here is a brief explanation of the phases of economic cycles according to Ray Dalio.

The short-term cycle, also known as the business cycle, is primarily regulated by central bank decisions. These institutions adjust their monetary policies by tightening them when inflation is high or rising significantly, and when credit growth is robust. Conversely, they ease their policies when economic conditions shift in the opposite direction.

Although different experts may describe these cycles in various ways, their underlying structure remains constant. Generally, these cycles unfold through six stages: four corresponding to the expansion phase and two to the recession phase.

When the expansion phase begins in the economy, there is initially an early-cycle stage. This stage typically lasts about 5 or 6 quarters. It starts with an increase in the demand for interest-sensitive goods, such as housing and automobiles. Retail sales tend to grow due to low interest rates and abundant credit availability. This rise in demand and production results in an improvement in employment. During this phase, credit expands rapidly, economic growth is vigorous (exceeding 4%), and inflation remains low. Consumption increases robustly, inventory accumulation rises, and the U.S. stock market often delivers the best returns, thanks to accelerated growth and stable interest rates due to controlled inflation. In contrast, inflation-linked assets and commodities tend to show lower performance.

Later, the intermediate cycle begins, lasting about 3 or 4 quarters. During this period, economic growth slows noticeably, settling around 2%. Inflation remains low, although consumption growth slows. Inventory accumulation begins to decrease, while interest rates tend to decline. As a result, stock market growth slows, and the decline in the value of inflation-linked assets moderates.

Following the intermediate cycle is the so-called late-cycle phase, which typically begins about two and a half years after the start of the expansion phase. At this point, economic growth stabilizes at moderate levels, between 3.5% and 4%. Although limitations in productive capacity begin to emerge, both credit and demand remain strong. Inflation starts to rise, consumption accelerates, and inventory accumulation increases. Interest rates rise, and the stock market reaches its final growth peaks. Inflation-linked assets stand out as the most attractive investments during this phase.

Finally, the compression phase arrives, where current or expected inflation leads the Federal Reserve to adopt a restrictive stance. This shift is manifested in reduced liquidity, an increase in interest rates, and a potential flattening or inversion of the yield curve. As a result, money supply and credit growth decline, causing stock markets to drop before there is a turnaround in the overall economy.

At this point, the expansion phase abruptly ends, and the so-called contraction phase begins. This phase is characterized by two clearly identifiable moments, starting with the so-called early recession phase. At this stage, the economy shows signs of contraction. Economic weakness is evident through indicators such as GDP, industrial capacity utilization, and the unemployment rate. The stock market, as well as commodity prices and inflation-linked assets, suffer declines due to the ongoing monetary tightening implemented by the Federal Reserve.

Following this initial stage of the recession, the late recession phase begins, where the central bank starts implementing expansive monetary policy measures. At this point, concerns about inflation become secondary, and recession worries dominate the scene. With lower interest rates, stock prices begin to rise, even though the economy has not yet shown clear signs of recovery. Meanwhile, commodity prices and inflation-linked assets continue to show weakness. The combination of low interest rates and rising stock prices sets the stage for the next expansion cycle.

As discussed, at Bridgewater, Dalio and his team develop strategies based on both quantitative and qualitative analysis of global economic data. The firm employs an "All Weather" investment approach, designed to perform positively in any economic environment, as previously explained. This strategy is based on extreme diversification and risk hedging, allowing Bridgewater to maintain stability even during times of high volatility.

The principles underlying the investment strategy with this portfolio are based on achieving broad exposure in both equity and bond markets to protect against significant declines during deleveraging periods.

This approach is effectively implemented through asset diversification, not only within different categories such as large-cap versus mid-cap stocks, or corporate versus government bonds, but also in terms of time horizon (short-term versus long-term).

Bridgewater's approach is based on a long-term perspective. Although the Bridgewater team constantly monitors markets and the economy, Dalio emphasizes that precise future predictions are impossible. Therefore, this portfolio is designed to protect against financial losses from unexpected economic events, known as black swans.

Portfolio diversification has long been a strategy to mitigate risk and volatility. The "All Weather" portfolio, according to its developers, employs a wide variety of asset classes to achieve optimal diversification. This diversification benefit partly arises from the uncorrelated nature of these assets, such that when stocks fall, bonds usually rise (although this has not always been the case).

The asset allocation in the "All Weather" portfolio is as follows:

30% U.S. stocks

40% long-term Treasury bonds

15% intermediate-term Treasury bonds

7.5% diversified commodities

7.5% gold

Due to fluctuations, this portfolio needs to be rebalanced, as the initial percentages will vary with these fluctuations. Thus, annually, different instruments will be bought or sold to return to the initial balance point.

Beyond his macroeconomic approach, Ray Dalio is perhaps best known for his set of principles, which he considers fundamental to success both in life and in business. These principles, compiled in his book titled "Principles: Life and Work," offer guidance for decision-making and problem-solving, not only in finance but in any aspect of life.

Dalio strongly believes in the meritocracy of ideas, where the best ideas should prevail regardless of their origin. At Bridgewater, this translates into a culture of extreme transparency and honesty, where all employees are encouraged to voice their opinions and where mistakes are seen as learning opportunities. This unique environment, which Dalio calls "idea meritocracy," is designed to challenge conventional thinking and foster innovation.

One of Dalio's key principles is the need to "face reality as it is, not as you would like it to be." This involves being brutally honest with oneself and others and being willing to change one's mind when the facts require it. Dalio also emphasizes the importance of learning from mistakes and constantly iterating to improve. This mindset of continuous growth has been fundamental to Bridgewater's success.

Furthermore, Ray Dalio proposes a systematic method for achieving success in life and business. This method consists of five fundamental steps that help you progress towards your goals through an evolutionary process:

The first step is to define clear goals. By setting specific objectives, you determine the direction in which you want to advance. Knowing exactly what you want to achieve provides you with a reference point and keeps you focused on what really matters.

Once you have your goals, it's important to identify the problems preventing you from reaching them. On the way to your objectives, you will inevitably encounter obstacles and difficulties. These problems are not signs of failure, but opportunities to learn and grow.

After recognizing the problems, it's essential to get to the root of each one. This means thoroughly analyzing what is causing those obstacles and understanding the underlying weaknesses or errors. Only by addressing the fundamental causes can you find effective solutions.

The next step is to design plans to overcome them. This involves creating specific and detailed strategies that address each root cause. A solid plan acts as a map that guides you toward solving your problems, allowing you to progress more efficiently toward your goals.

Finally, it is crucial to implement your plans with discipline and determination. Execution is where many people fall short, as putting a plan into practice requires perseverance and commitment.

Another fundamental principle emphasized by Ray Dalio is maintaining an open mindset as a crucial trait for success in life. There are two major barriers that prevent this: your ego and your blind spots. The first refers to the inability to recognize our own weaknesses and the reluctance to have others point them out. The second refers to all the information we are unaware exists, which leads to suboptimal decisions due to a lack of knowledge. These two barriers prevent you from seeing reality objectively. Radical open-mindedness helps you overcome this. It allows you to make optimal decisions by avoiding the traps of your ego or blind spots. It requires replacing the notion of always being right with the desire to learn what is true, or at least getting as close as possible to the truth, acknowledging that absolute truth does not exist.

On the other hand, in Ray Dalio's book "Principles," he describes himself as a "professional decision-maker," a skill he has refined throughout his career. Dalio argues that many of the decisions we make daily are made at a subconscious level, which can be challenging when it comes to making decisions in a reliable, systematic, and repeatable manner. To help others improve their decision-making process, Dalio offers a series of practical tips that can guide people toward more effective decisions.

First, Dalio emphasizes the importance of recognizing that emotions are often the biggest threat to good decision-making. He suggests that decisions should be viewed as a two-step process: first, learn everything you can about the situation, and then make an informed decision. By doing so, you can mitigate the impact of emotions on the process.

Next, Dalio recommends synthesizing the current situation, meaning identifying the key factors relevant to the decision-making process. This also includes the need to synthesize the situation over time, observing how different factors behave to gain a more complete understanding of their nature.

Another crucial aspect is the ability to change perspective. This involves being able to see both the big picture and the more subtle details of the situation, allowing for a more comprehensive and balanced evaluation.

He also advises relying on logic, reasoning, and common sense to gain the best possible understanding of reality. This is fundamental to avoid having decisions affected by biases or unfounded assumptions. Furthermore, each decision should be approached as a value calculation, evaluating the likelihood of it being right or wrong and considering the possible outcomes.

A key point in the decision-making process is determining when it is necessary to prioritize acquiring more information and when it is more valuable to act quickly. Simplifying the process by eliminating superfluous information can help avoid analysis paralysis.

Dalio highlights the importance of using clear principles to guide the decision-making process. These principles can become algorithms, allowing decisions to be made in a more objective and consistent manner.

Finally, Dalio underscores the importance of considering credibility when making decisions. This involves seeking the opinions of intelligent and reliable experts before committing to a final decision, which can provide valuable perspective and avoid costly mistakes.

As we can see from the previous paragraphs, Ray Dalio is a macro investor with a highly developed critical sense. After failing in his investing career, he decided not to leave many of the variables affecting both investment and achieving life goals to chance. Undoubtedly, Ray Dalio is characterized by his flexibility, which allows him to adapt to new circumstances, whether economic or experiential. For all these reasons, as investors, we should look to a figure like Ray Dalio to approach investing with humility and, above all, with the curiosity that novices have when facing their first investments.

BENJAMIN GRAHAM: THE FATHER OF VALUE INVESTING

Although Benjamin Graham is no longer alive, his significance in the investment world is substantial enough to warrant discussion in these pages. Graham is considered the "Father of Value Investing" and a fundamental figure in finance. His methodical and analytical approach has left an indelible mark on the way investors think about the markets. Graham's life and work not only transformed the field of investing but also inspired generations of investors, including his most famous student, Warren Buffett.

Benjamin Graham was born Benjamin Grossbaum on May 9, 1894, in London, England. His family emigrated to the United States when he was a child, settling in New York. The family changed their surname from Grossbaum to Graham to better assimilate into American culture and escape the prevalent antisemitism of the time. Although his family enjoyed a brief period of economic prosperity, the collapse of their business after his father's death plunged them into poverty, which deeply affected Graham.

Despite the financial hardships, Graham excelled in his studies and earned a scholarship to attend Columbia University, graduating with honors in 1914. Graham was an exceptional student, excelling in a wide range of disciplines, from philosophy to mathematics. After graduation, he was offered positions in the English, mathematics, and philosophy departments but chose to work on Wall Street, where he began his career in finance.

Graham's career on Wall Street led him to develop the investment approach known as value investing, a philosophy he considered both a science and an art. As we have seen, this approach focuses on buying stocks that are trading below their intrinsic value.

Graham argued that the stock market is often irrational, subject to emotional highs and lows that can lead to overvaluation or undervaluation of individual stocks. This approach contrasts with trend-based investing, which focuses on capitalizing on market ups and downs. Graham maintained that investors should focus on a thorough analysis of a company's financial statements, considering factors such as earnings, expenses, assets, and debts.

Perhaps Benjamin Graham was not the first to present such ideas, which in some ways were a novel way of understanding investing; however, he was one of the investors who made the most effort to equip new investors with the knowledge needed to navigate the investment world confidently. This led to the creation of two of the most important works in investment history: the book "Security Analysis," published in 1934 and co-written with David Dodd, where he established the fundamental principles of value investing and provided a detailed framework for analyzing and valuing stocks, and the book "The Intelligent Investor," which has been hailed as one of the best books on investing ever written. In this book, Graham outlines his ideas on how investors can protect themselves from significant errors and learn to develop long-term strategies.

In the following pages, we will examine his second work, "The Intelligent Investor," which encompasses all the wisdom of value investing that every investor should know.

Value investing is based on identifying investment opportunities where the true value of a stock is higher than the price paid for it. Graham maintained that stocks with a Price-to-Earnings Ratio (P/E Ratio) below 10 represent interesting opportunities for investors. As we have seen, the P/E Ratio is a financial metric calculated by dividing the stock price by the earnings per share. A low P/E suggests that the stock might be undervalued relative to its earnings.

Moreover, Graham emphasized that success in investing does not come from seeking immediate gains, but from adopting a long-term perspective. Investors should conduct thorough analyses to identify a portfolio of undervalued stocks with growth potential. This requires detailed analysis of financial statements and company balances to determine if they are viable and promising in the long term.

Once the stocks are purchased, it is essential to have the patience to wait for the market to recognize their true value. This approach contrasts with short-term market fluctuations, which can lead to temporary undervaluation of stocks, resulting in potential losses for impatient investors.

On the other hand, Graham makes a crucial distinction between speculation and investing, two concepts often confused. An investor acts as if they are a part-owner of a company. This approach involves a long-term commitment to the company and a genuine interest in its success and profitability. The investor is willing to wait for returns, trusting that thorough analysis and careful selection of undervalued stocks will pay off over time. In contrast, a speculator is driven by the pursuit of quick profits, without deeply considering the characteristics and potential of the company they invest in. Speculation can lead to catastrophic results and significant losses if bets do not turn out as expected. Graham advocates for an investment approach based on security and reliable long-term results, rather than seeking quick gains through speculation.

In his book, Graham describes two types of intelligent investors: the passive (or defensive) investor and the active (or aggressive) investor. Both types can succeed, but their approaches and objectives are different. Passive investors focus on avoiding significant mistakes and losses. They prefer not to spend too much time selecting assets and seek to minimize the risk of errors. Their approach is generally more conservative and designed to protect capital rather than maximize profits. On the other hand, active investors devote considerable time and effort to finding the best investment opportunities. They are willing to take on more risks and strive to achieve returns that outperform the market. According to Graham, with patience and dedication, active investors can achieve significant benefits, though this requires a substantial commitment of time and resources for analysis and asset selection.

The stock market is known for its volatile and unpredictable nature. Stock prices can fluctuate rapidly due to a range of factors, from global economic changes to the emotional state of investors. Graham used the metaphor of "Mr. Market" to describe this phenomenon. He imagined "Mr. Market" as a character who swings between unchecked optimism and deep pessimism. When "Mr. Market" is in a good mood, stock prices are high, while in his pessimistic state, they are sold at low prices.

For Graham, the intelligent investor is one who can benefit from these mood swings by buying stocks when "Mr. Market" is depressed and offers them at bargain prices, and selling them when he is euphoric and offers them at high prices. By understanding market phases and staying calm during fluctuations, investors can make more rational decisions and avoid common mistakes of panic selling or euphoric buying during peaks of optimism.

One of the key concepts in Graham's book is known as the "margin of safety." As we have seen, this margin refers to the difference between a stock's intrinsic value and its market price. By buying stocks that are significantly below their intrinsic value, investors can protect themselves against errors and market fluctuations. The margin of safety acts as a safety net, ensuring that even if the market declines or calculation errors occur, potential losses are minimized.

Graham advises investors not to attempt to predict market movements, but to focus on finding undervalued stocks with a wide margin of safety. This not only helps to protect capital but also provides an opportunity to achieve significant gains when the market eventually recognizes the true value of these stocks.

Another pillar of Graham's approach is diversification. He advises investors not to put all their capital into a single stock, no matter how promising it may seem. Diversification among different stocks and mutual funds reduces the risk of significant losses if a single company encounters problems.

Graham suggests that investors should maintain a balance between stocks and bonds. Generally, he recommends not having more than 75% of the capital invested in stocks, allocating the remainder to bonds. This strategy can offer peace of mind by reducing portfolio volatility, even though stocks tend to provide higher returns over the long term. Diversification not only protects capital but also allows investors to capitalize on various growth opportunities in the market.

Another concept Graham emphasizes in his book is inflation, meaning the general increase in the prices of goods and services. This rise is a constant concern for investors, and according to Graham, one of the best ways to protect against inflation is to invest in solid, carefully selected stocks. Although inflation erodes purchasing power, stocks can offer returns that outpace the inflation rate, preserving and increasing the value of investors' wealth.

The success of an investment is measured by the growth of net worth after accounting for inflation. Graham argues that by carefully selecting stocks and holding them long-term, investors can counteract the negative impact of inflation on their personal finances.

From this information, a series of key lessons for investors can be extracted, which we will delve into through Graham's famous quotes:

"Any purchase of a security should be justifiable both qualitatively and quantitatively." Here, Graham emphasizes the importance of conducting a thorough analysis before investing. Investors should examine both qualitative aspects, such as the business model and the quality of the management team, and quantitative aspects, such as financial statements and valuation metrics. Only by buying stocks with a solid foundation on both fronts can one minimize risk and maximize return potential.

"Financial intelligence is more a trait of character than of intellect." Graham highlights that financial intelligence goes beyond technical knowledge. It includes traits like discipline, patience, and emotional control. People with financial intelligence can resist the temptation to react impulsively to market fluctuations and stay true to their long-term strategy. It is important to mentally prepare for the battleground that is stock price fluctuation. Stock volatility can play tricks on us, and it is better to view this situation as an intrinsic part of investing, focusing on other factors rather than daily stock quotes.

"The intelligent investor knows that stocks become riskier as their prices rise and less risky as prices fall." This principle goes against common intuition, which often perceives stocks as less risky as their prices go up. However, Graham teaches that risk increases with overvaluation, while price declines can present attractive buying opportunities if the company's fundamentals are sound. We should never forget this assertion when the stocks we own drop 50% in the market. During these difficult times, we must remember that if our investment thesis has not changed, the implicit risk of the investment is lower than when we started buying, and thus we should not fear the decline. Moreover, if we have more capital, we should continue buying shares of the company.

"The market is like a pendulum that swings between unsustainable optimism (which makes assets too expensive) and unjustified pessimism (which makes assets too cheap). The intelligent investor is a realist who sells to optimists and buys from pessimists." Graham illustrates the market as a pendulum swinging between extremes. Intelligent investors know how to take advantage of these movements, buying when prices are low due to pessimism and selling when optimism drives prices too high. Understanding the market pendulum is crucial, as when we think a stock cannot drop further, the harsh reality often proves this assumption wrong. Therefore, it is important to be aware that the market can go haywire temporarily and crush the prices of many companies. Being psychologically prepared for this eventuality can save us some headaches.

"Investing is smarter the more it resembles running a business." For Graham, effective investing should be approached with the same seriousness and strategic focus as managing a business. This involves thorough analysis, long-term planning, and constant evaluation of risks and opportunities. Many investors treat investing like a game of chance, when it is actually a business operation. Stocks give us the chance to buy parts of businesses with a small amount of capital, which would otherwise be impossible. For this reason, we should act like a small business owner who invests capital in buying businesses, with stocks being the means to do so.

"Achieving satisfactory investment results is easier than most people think; achieving superior results is more difficult than it seems." Finally, Graham indicates that obtaining reasonable investment results is accessible with a disciplined and well-informed approach. However, consistently outperforming the market requires a much higher level of skill, analysis, and discipline. This statement underscores the importance of setting realistic expectations and valuing the long term over quick gains. We should not view investing as a fast track to wealth, but rather as a means to gradually grow our capital and, over time, accumulate enough to be free from daily economic problems.

It is important to highlight that Benjamin Graham's influence on Warren Buffett is undeniable. Buffett's fascination with stocks led him to discover Benjamin Graham's book, "The Intelligent Investor." This text, considered a bible of value investing, introduced Buffett to key concepts like the margin of safety and intrinsic value evaluation.

Buffett was so impressed by Graham's ideas that he decided to study under his guidance at Columbia Business School. After graduating, he worked for Graham at his investment firm, Graham-Newman Corporation. During this time, Buffett absorbed Graham's teachings, learning to identify undervalued stocks and apply a rigorous analytical approach to investing.

From Graham, Buffett learned to seek stocks whose market price was below their intrinsic value, calculated through thorough analysis of financial statements and business potential. Additionally, Buffett applied the fundamental concept of the "margin of safety" and, of course, learned the importance of patience, waiting for the right moment to buy stocks when the market presented significant opportunities.

However, Buffett's initial influence from Graham evolved over the years. As he famously expressed, "It is better to buy a wonderful company at a fair price than a fair company at a wonderful price." This statement contradicts some of Benjamin Graham's teachings, as Buffett, while developing his career, met Charlie Munger, who would later become his partner and Vice Chairman of Berkshire Hathaway. Munger, with his intellectual and multidisciplinary approach, brought a new perspective to Buffett's investment process.

Munger encouraged Buffett to seek high-quality companies with sustainable competitive advantages, even if they were not significantly undervalued. This new approach led Warren Buffett to invest in companies that were fairly priced but had the capacity to grow and maintain their competitive edge over the years.

The combined influence of Graham and Munger resulted in a unique approach to investing, where Buffett achieved a synthesis between Graham's rigorous quantitative analysis and Munger's qualitative and more holistic approach. This hybrid philosophy allowed him to identify opportunities that other investors might have overlooked, enabling him to become, arguably, the greatest investor in history.

JOHN BOGLE: THE PIONEER OF INDEXED INVESTING

John Bogle, known as the father of indexed investing, had a profound impact on the financial world by democratizing access to the markets for individual investors. His focus on simplicity, frugality, and discipline changed the way people invest and helped transform the investment management industry.

John Clifton Bogle was born on May 8, 1929, in Montclair, New Jersey, into a family that suffered the aftermath of the Great Depression. This experience influenced his perspective on money and investing, instilling in him an appreciation for frugality and saving from an early age. Bogle attended Blair Academy in Blairstown, New Jersey, and later entered Princeton University, where he graduated with honors in 1951 with a degree in economics.

In his undergraduate thesis, Bogle investigated the investment fund industry, a topic that piqued his interest and laid the foundation for his future career. In his work, he highlighted the inefficiencies and high costs of actively managed funds and suggested the idea of an investment fund that would simply replicate the market's performance rather than trying to beat it.

After graduating, Bogle began his career at Wellington Management Company, an investment management firm, where he quickly rose to become president in 1967. However, a series of strategic missteps led to his dismissal in 1974, which turned out to be a turning point in his professional life.

Determined to learn from his mistakes and create a new approach to investing, Bogle founded The Vanguard Group in 1975. It was here that he began to implement his ideas about indexed investing, a concept that would revolutionize the investment fund industry.

Unlike many of the investors we've seen, who are known for active investing, John Bogle's investment philosophy focused on simplicity and efficiency. Through Vanguard, he launched the first index fund available to individual investors, the Vanguard 500 Index Fund, in 1976. The idea behind an index fund is simple: instead of trying to outperform the market by actively selecting stocks, the fund seeks to replicate the performance of a specific market index, such as the S&P 500, thereby creating one of the first passive investment funds.

After years in the investment world, Bogle believed that the high costs of actively managed funds were a barrier to long-term returns. By replicating an index, index funds can operate with significantly lower costs since they do not require a team of investment managers analyzing and selecting stocks. Additionally, index funds offer broad diversification by investing in all the stocks within an index. This reduces company-specific risk and allows investors to benefit from overall market growth over time.

In this way, Bogle advocated for long-term investing while discouraging speculative investing, which is more akin to gambling than to genuine investing. He believed that staying invested in the market over time was the best way to generate consistent wealth without complication.

Unlike most other investors, Bogle believed that markets are generally efficient, meaning that most available information is already reflected in stock prices. Therefore, consistently beating the market is extremely difficult and often costly, making indexed investing a simple and straightforward way to achieve significant returns.

Today, indexed investing has become one of the most important investment strategies, both in terms of the number of investors and the amount of capital invested. Undoubtedly, the great accessibility and simplicity of indexed investing have led millions of investors to avoid unnecessary complications and understand that wealth accumulates over time. For some of the greatest investors in history, indexed investing has become a safe bet, while for others, it is seen as one of the major bubbles in the investment world.

However, this was not always the case; initially, the concept of index funds was met with skepticism and resistance from the investment management industry. Many professionals considered the idea of merely matching the market rather than trying to beat it to be a mediocre approach. Nevertheless, over time, empirical evidence demonstrated that few active managers consistently outperformed their benchmarks after accounting for costs.

As investors began to recognize the benefits of index funds, Bogle's approach gained popularity. Today, index funds represent a significant portion of assets under management worldwide, and Vanguard has become one of the largest asset managers in the world.

Thus, one of John Bogle's greatest contributions to the world of investing is what is known as the "democratization" of investing. Bogle's commitment was to make investing accessible to everyone, regardless of their level of wealth. Low-cost index funds allowed individual investors to participate in the growth of financial markets in a cost-effective and straightforward manner. Today, thanks to Bogle, no one has an excuse not to invest in a simple, quick, and low-cost way. Everyone should invest at least a portion of their capital in index funds as a fundamental strategy for growing their money while also protecting against the adverse effects of inflation.

Bogle's insights are captured in many of the phrases he provided in numerous media interviews or through his bestselling book, "The Little Book of Common Sense Investing."

"Learn every day. But most importantly, learn from the experiences of others. It's cheaper!" This phrase captures the essence of Bogle's pragmatic approach to life and investing. For him, continuous learning is crucial, but even more important is learning from the mistakes and successes of others. In the world of investing, where decisions can have significant consequences, absorbing the accumulated knowledge of other investors and avoiding repeating their mistakes is a way of saving not just money but also time and energy.

Bogle understood that financial markets are full of lessons, many of them painful. That is why he insisted that investors should study market history and the experiences of other investors to anticipate the challenges they might face. By learning from others' falls and mistakes, one can avoid making the same errors and better protect their capital.

This philosophy of learning from others is also reflected in how Bogle built Vanguard and popularized index funds. He observed how actively managed funds often failed to outperform the market after accounting for their high costs and fees. Instead of trying to compete with these funds, he decided to offer an alternative that learned from the mistakes of active management: a fund that simply replicated the market rather than trying to beat it. Thus, the first index fund available to the public was born, an innovation that is now a cornerstone in the investment strategies of many investors.

His commitment to index fund investing is encapsulated in another of his famous quotes: "Forget the needle, buy the haystack. Buy the whole market and you can eliminate stock risk, style risk, and manager risk. Your chances of finding the next Apple are slim." This phrase is a brilliant metaphor that encapsulates Bogle's investment philosophy. The "needle" represents high-performance stocks, those few companies that achieve explosive growth and generate enormous returns for their investors. However, as Bogle points out, the chances of identifying these companies before they achieve their success are extremely low. Instead of spending time and resources trying to find these "needles," Bogle suggests that it is much wiser to "buy the haystack," meaning investing in the entire market.

Investing in the entire market through an index fund is a strategy that eliminates several types of risks that Bogle considered unnecessary. The risks of individual stocks, style risk, and manager risk are factors that can destabilize an investment portfolio. By investing in a fund that replicates the entire market, an investor can mitigate these risks, as their exposure is automatically diversified across hundreds or thousands of companies. This not only reduces the impact of any single company that fails to meet expectations but also, as we've discussed, ensures that the investor benefits from the overall market growth over time.

Bogle also understood that many investors are tempted by the desire to find the next big company, the next "Apple." However, he knew that this approach is more akin to playing the lottery than to investing wisely. His advice was clear: do not chase unreachable dreams when you can secure a solid and reliable return by investing in the entire market.

Although Bogle's style was quite different from other investors, there is something common among all of them: time and patience. "Time is your friend, impulse is your enemy. Patience is the most important gift of the investor. Embrace it, take advantage of compound interest, and don't be seduced by the siren songs of the market." Patience is a recurring theme in

Bogle's teachings, and this phrase summarizes why he considered it vital for investment success. In a world where the market can fluctuate wildly from one day to the next, Bogle understood that investors needed to resist the temptation to react impulsively to these fluctuations. Time, Bogle said, is an investor's greatest ally because it allows the effects of compound interest to work in their favor.

Compound interest is one of the most powerful forces in finance, and Bogle was a staunch advocate of making the most of it. When investors allow their returns to generate more returns, they can accumulate considerable wealth over time, even with a modest growth rate. However, this process requires patience and discipline, qualities that Bogle deeply valued.

The "impulse" Bogle refers to is that constant pressure investors feel to act, to do something, especially in response to market news or daily fluctuations in stock prices. Even in the absence of these forces, many investors believe that inactivity is not part of investing, which is often one of the major mistakes new investors make in their early years, perceiving investing as a world full of frenetic activity. As the wise Charlie Munger said, "The big money is not in the buying and selling, but in the waiting."

Like Charlie, Bogle believed that this impulse was one of the greatest enemies of an investor. The key, in his view, was to remain calm and keep focused on the long term, resisting the siren calls that might divert investors from their path.

On the other hand, for Bogle, "The secret to investing is that there is no secret. When you own the entire stock market through a broad market index fund with an appropriate allocation and a global bond index fund, you have the optimal investment strategy." One of Bogle's most notable characteristics was his aversion to unnecessary complexity. In a financial world full of gurus and experts offering supposedly secret and miraculous investment strategies, Bogle offered a refreshing perspective: there is no secret to successful investing. His approach was straightforward and accessible, based on proven and simple principles.

For Bogle, the optimal investment strategy was to own the entire market through a broad index fund, combined with an appropriate allocation in a global bond index fund. This strategy provided diversification, low costs, and a passive approach that, over time, outperformed most active managers who attempted to beat the market. The simplicity of this strategy is precisely what makes it so effective. Bogle argued that the search for secrets or complex strategies often leads investors down dangerous paths.

These paths are not only more expensive but can also expose investors to unnecessary risks.

During his investment career, Bogle observed how renowned fund managers would appear on top-performing lists for five years and then suddenly return to mediocre results, making way for other managers who had not been previously mentioned. According to Bogle, "You will never find a fund manager who consistently beats the market. That's why it's better to invest in an index fund that allows you to capture market returns while paying lower fees."

As Bogle clearly demonstrated, he was a staunch critic of active management, which, according to him, rarely justified its high costs. Most fund managers, he argued, could not consistently outperform the market over time. This is because, after accounting for fees and expenses, the net returns of these funds often fall short compared to the overall market performance.

Additionally, it is common for major fund managers to hold the same stocks that are already among the top holdings of index funds. This occurs due to a combination of factors. Firstly, some managers handle enormous amounts of capital, making it impossible to invest in smaller companies, and to have a significant position, they must invest in companies with high capitalization, which coincidentally are the same ones with the largest weight in index funds.

On the other hand, over time, managers often develop conservative strategies out of fear of making mistakes. Many top investors tend to invest in the same companies as other managers so that if they make a mistake, it can be more easily justified than if they had invested in a company no one else held in their portfolio. This clearly reflects the saying "Misery loves company." While it might surprise readers, it's enough to analyze the portfolios of various investors to quickly notice how the same companies keep appearing.

Therefore, it seems reasonable that if most managers invest in the same companies, and these are heavily represented in any of the indices used for passive investing, it is more profitable and less costly to invest in such instruments. By replicating the market instead of trying to beat it, index funds offered investors a way to ensure market returns while keeping costs low. This combination, according to Bogle, was a winning formula for long-term investors.

Bogle's insistence on low costs and simplicity not only helped popularize index funds but also pressured the fund management industry to reconsider its business models. Today, largely due to Bogle's influence, investors have access to a wide range of low-cost investment options that allow them to participate in market growth without sacrificing a significant portion of their returns in fees.

As we have mentioned, John Bogle profoundly changed the world of investing, opening up the investment landscape so that ordinary people could invest in a simple and low-cost manner. At the same time, Bogle urged investors to have moderate expectations about market returns. Many investors have become some of the wealthiest people in the world thanks to investing, but we must be clear about this point, as they are the exception rather than the rule. Investing, with its inherent risks and dreams of great wealth, has evaporated the money of many investors who approached investing imprudently. That is why, now more than ever, the passive investing approach that John Bogle popularized remains one of the most important, easiest to follow, and undoubtedly most effective strategies.

BILL ACKMAN: ACTIVISM AND PERSUASION

Bill Ackman is a prominent figure in the financial world, known for his bold and controversial approach to activist investing. His career exemplifies how persuasion and activism can be combined to influence the fate of large corporations, and his story is a lesson on how determination and a clear vision can alter the course of companies and markets.

William Albert Ackman, known as Bill Ackman, was born on May 11, 1966, in Chappaqua, New York, into a well-to-do Jewish family. His father, Lawrence Ackman, was the president of a New York real estate firm, giving Ackman early access to the business and finance world. He studied history at Harvard University, where he earned his undergraduate degree, and then completed an MBA at Harvard Business School. His education at one of the world's most prestigious universities was just the first step toward a career that would redefine activism in investing.

Bill Ackman's investment strategy is rooted in activism. Unlike traditional investors who buy shares for passive gains, Ackman seeks to actively influence the management and direction of the companies in which he invests. His approach involves acquiring significant stakes in companies he believes are mismanaged or undervalued, and then pressuring for strategic changes to unlock their hidden value. This method often involves direct confrontations with the senior management and board of directors of the companies, and has led to Ackman being viewed both as a savior and a villain, depending on the perspective.

Moreover, Ackman distinguishes himself from other activist investors with his persuasive style and ability to articulate his vision not only to company executives but also to shareholders and the public. He is a master at using the media to garner support for his cause and often presents his investment theses in a detailed and public manner, which allows him to apply pressure on companies to implement his suggestions. This ability to persuade is one of Ackman's most powerful tools, enabling him to mobilize both investors and public opinion in his favor.

This type of investing is not feasible for individual investors who invest their savings in specific companies, but through Bill Ackman, we can learn how the business world functions and how sometimes poor management by a company's leadership can harm its shareholders.

In these pages, we will highlight two of his successful investments that exemplify Bill Ackman's adeptness as an activist investor. In 2011, Ackman turned his attention to Canadian Pacific Railway (CP), one of North America's major railroads. Despite its history and significance in the industry, Canadian Pacific was experiencing a period of poor performance, reflected in operational inefficiencies and a lack of growth. For Ackman, the situation was clear: the company had enormous untapped potential but was being poorly managed.

With the firm belief that a change in leadership could revitalize the company, Ackman, through his firm Pershing Square Capital Management, acquired a significant stake in Canadian Pacific. This initial move was only the beginning of what would become an intense and prolonged battle for control of the company.

Ackman began his campaign by pressuring the board of directors of Canadian Pacific to make significant management changes. At the heart of his strategy was the idea of replacing CEO Fred Green, whom Ackman considered ineffective in taking the company to the next level. He argued that the current management was not only failing to exploit Canadian Pacific's potential but was also leaving the company lagging behind its competitors.

Resistance to Ackman's proposed changes was fierce. Canadian Pacific's management, supported by some board members, strongly opposed Green's removal. The battle intensified when Ackman launched a public campaign to gain the support of other shareholders, presenting his vision for the company's future and emphasizing the need for new leadership.

After months of disputes and intense exchanges of opinion, Ackman finally achieved his goal. Fred Green was replaced by Hunter Harrison, a veteran of the railroad industry with a proven reputation for success at Canadian National Railway. Under Harrison's leadership, the transformation of Canadian Pacific was rapid and remarkable. A series of operational reforms were implemented that drastically improved the company's efficiency, reduced costs, and increased profitability.

Within a few years, the company's value skyrocketed, and shareholders saw a significant return on their investment. This success not only solidified Canadian Pacific as a leading player in the railroad industry but also strengthened Ackman's reputation as an effective and visionary activist, capable of taking control of complex situations and delivering positive results.

Another notable episode in Ackman's career was his intervention in Allergan, a pharmaceutical company known for products like Botox. In 2014, Ackman partnered with Valeant Pharmaceuticals in an attempt to make a hostile takeover of Allergan. This strategic move was innovative and controversial, as it involved collaboration between an activist investor and a pharmaceutical company to acquire another company in the same sector.

Ackman's strategy was simple but bold: to purchase a large amount of Allergan shares before publicly announcing Valeant's intention to acquire the company. This approach, while legal, was highly controversial and sparked a significant debate about Ackman's tactics. However, the operation was not as straightforward as Ackman and Valeant had hoped. Allergan's board of directors vehemently opposed the takeover offer, arguing that it was insufficient and significantly undervalued the company. Instead of accepting Valeant's offer, Allergan began exploring alternatives, leading to a counteroffer from Actavis, a rival pharmaceutical company.

Despite the resistance, Ackman and Valeant continued to push, convinced they could win the battle for control of Allergan. The dispute intensified, with both the media and financial markets closely following the situation. In a move that surprised many, Actavis made a substantially higher offer to acquire Allergan, an offer that was accepted by Allergan's board of directors.

Although Ackman and Valeant did not achieve their initial goal of acquiring Allergan, Ackman once again demonstrated his ability to create value even in adverse situations. After Actavis announced its acquisition, Allergan's stock value rose significantly. Ackman, who had bought a considerable stake in Allergan before Valeant's offer was announced, sold his shares with a substantial profit, achieving a financial victory even in an apparent strategic defeat.

However, not all of Ackman's activist investments ended well. His most famous activist investment to date is the one he made in Herbalife. Undoubtedly, Bill Ackman's campaign against Herbalife became one of the most controversial and polarizing episodes in recent Wall Street history. Known for his combative style and activist approach, Ackman bet big against the nutritional supplements and weight control products company, accusing it of operating as a pyramid scheme that would inevitably collapse. This confrontation not only tested Ackman's reputation and skills as an investor but also attracted the attention of regulators, media, and other giants of the financial industry.

In December 2012, Ackman, through his hedge fund Pershing Square Capital Management, made an unprecedented public accusation against Herbalife, claiming that the company was nothing more than a disguised pyramid scheme. According to Ackman, Herbalife did not generate its income primarily from selling products to end consumers, but from continually recruiting new distributors who bought products to meet their sales quotas and advance in the company's hierarchical system. In his view, this business model was unsustainable and, like all pyramid schemes, would eventually collapse.

Ackman did not limit himself to making public statements; he went much further. He organized a three-hour presentation in New York, where he detailed his case against Herbalife with meticulous detail. The presentation, titled "Is Herbalife a Pyramid Scheme?", included charts, testimonies from former distributors, and a thorough analysis of the company's financial statements. Ackman argued that the vast majority of Herbalife's distributors did not make money, but instead suffered significant losses while trying to meet the sales targets set by the company.

In addition to the presentation, Ackman took his campaign to the media. He appeared on financial news programs, wrote opinion pieces, and used all available platforms to spread his message: Herbalife was deceiving thousands of people, and it was only a matter of time before authorities intervened and the company would collapse.

Ackman put his money where his mouth was. He invested one billion dollars in a short position against Herbalife, meaning he bet that the company's stock price would fall. His prediction was clear: once the market understood the true nature of Herbalife's business, the stock would plummet, and his bet would be incredibly profitable.

Ackman's decision was bold and risky. Not only did he bet a massive amount of money, but he did so very publicly. Herbalife's response was swift and fierce. The company categorically denied Ackman's accusations, defending its business model and the legitimacy of its practices. Herbalife argued that its business was based on the sale of high-quality products and that many of its distributors were satisfied and making profits. The company also hired top legal and public relations advisors to counter Ackman's campaign and restore investor confidence.

What followed was a prolonged battle involving not only Herbalife and Ackman, but also other prominent figures on Wall Street. One of Ackman's most notable rivals was Carl Icahn, a well-known activist investor with a long history of corporate confrontations. Icahn saw an opportunity to challenge Ackman and began buying shares of Herbalife, betting that the company would survive the campaign against it.

The confrontation between Ackman and Icahn became a media spectacle. The two billionaires exchanged insults and faced off publicly on television programs. Icahn, in particular, became a vocal supporter of Herbalife, asserting that the company had a solid future and that Ackman was completely mistaken.

After years of struggle, in 2018, Ackman decided to close his short position in Herbalife. Despite his initial firm conviction, the campaign had become a costly distraction for Pershing Square, both in terms of financial resources and time and energy. Herbalife's stock price not only failed to collapse but remained surprisingly stable and even increased during certain periods. The closure of the position marked one of the most visible defeats in Ackman's career. However, Ackman remained firm in his belief that he was right about the nature of Herbalife's business, although he acknowledged that he underestimated the company's ability to withstand the pressure.

Years later, Bill Ackman would acknowledge his significant mistake. This mistake was not in exposing the possible fraud that Herbalife was perpetrating with its distributors, but in betting against the company's stock. Ackman realized that in the investment world, one should seek asymmetric bets, where risk is minimized and reward is maximized. By betting against Herbalife's stock, Ackman could only have gained 100% of the invested capital while potentially losing much more than 100%. However, by betting long, or in favor of the stock price rising, we might lose 100% of our invested capital but could gain much more than that 100%.

In his famous quote, "Failure is simply the opportunity to begin again, this time more intelligently," he encapsulated the lessons that come with such errors. Years later, a much smarter Bill Ackman made what has been to date the most beneficial investment in history.

At the beginning of 2020, the world was beginning to realize the severity of the COVID-19 outbreak, which was rapidly spreading from China to other parts of the globe. However, most financial markets had not yet fully reacted to the potential threat of a global pandemic. Nonetheless, Bill Ackman was one of the few people on Wall Street who quickly recognized the devastating impact that the virus could have on the global economy. As reports about COVID-19 became more alarming, Ackman began to consider how to protect Pershing Square's portfolio from the anticipated economic impact. That's when he decided on Credit Default Swaps (CDS).

CDS are a type of financial instrument that functions as a form of insurance against credit default. Essentially, an investor who buys a CDS is betting that a certain debt, whether from a company, a country, or a set of assets, might default. If the default occurs, the investor who purchased the CDS receives a payment that compensates for the loss. Therefore, CDS can be extremely profitable in times of crisis, when the risk of default increases dramatically.

In this case, Ackman saw that the spread of COVID-19 could lead to an economic collapse that would endanger the stability of many companies and governments. If this scenario materialized, the prices of CDS would rise significantly, allowing Ackman to earn substantial sums of money.

As the pandemic intensified, Ackman decided to act quickly. Through Pershing Square, he acquired CDS valued at approximately $27 million, betting that the credit market would experience a significant correction due to the impact of COVID-19. While $27 million might seem like a considerable amount, it was a relatively small investment compared to the total size of Pershing Square's portfolio, which managed billions of dollars at that time. However, the potential profitability was enormous, demonstrating asymmetric investment, and Ackman was willing to risk that amount of money based on his belief that his calculations were correct.

Ackman's move turned out to be a massive financial success. As COVID-19 spread and global economies went into recession, the CDS Ackman had acquired increased significantly in value. By the end of March, Pershing Square had turned its initial $27 million investment into a return of $2.6 billion, an impressive gain that catapulted Ackman into the spotlight as one of the few fund managers who had anticipated and capitalized on the crisis.

After securing this profit, Ackman liquidated his position in the CDS and used the gains to reinvest in companies he believed would survive and thrive after the pandemic. He bought shares in companies such as Starbucks, Hilton, and Lowe's, betting on their long-term recovery. This decision demonstrated Ackman's flexibility as an investor, capable of quickly adapting to changing circumstances and seizing opportunities in both declining and recovering markets, undoubtedly making him one of the greatest and most spectacular investors in history.

STANLEY DRUCKENMILLER: MACRO AND MARKETS

Stanley Druckenmiller is one of the most legendary investors in the world, known for his macroeconomic approach and his ability to read and anticipate global trends in financial markets. Throughout his career, he has demonstrated a unique capacity to identify and capitalize on major economic movements, becoming a benchmark in the investment world.

Stanley Druckenmiller was born on June 14, 1953, in Pittsburgh, Pennsylvania. Raised in a middle-class family, his life was not initially marked by luxury or opulence. Despite his modest beginnings, he excelled in his studies and showed a great aptitude for analysis and strategic thinking.

Druckenmiller attended Bowdoin College in Maine, where he graduated in Economics and English in 1975. He then began a Ph.D. program in Economics at the University of Michigan, but his fate took an unexpected turn when he left the program to accept a position at Pittsburgh National Bank as a petroleum analyst in 1977. From that moment, his career began to take shape, and he quickly stood out for his ability to understand the complexities of the market and the global economy.

What sets Stanley Druckenmiller apart from other investors is his macroeconomic approach, a strategy that focuses on analyzing global economic trends and how they influence financial markets. In Druckenmiller's own words, "Profits don't move the market overall; it's the Federal Reserve Board."

Unlike investors who specialize in analyzing individual companies or specific sectors, Druckenmiller has always looked at the big picture, focusing on monetary policies, changes in interest rates, currency fluctuations, and other macroeconomic factors.

Druckenmiller has stated on several occasions that, for him, the key to successful investing is capital preservation and taking calculated risks only when the odds are clearly in his favor. One of his most well-known philosophies is that "the best opportunities come when investors are most scared," which has allowed him to benefit from market panics and corrections.

Druckenmiller's view of the market has been shaped by his ability to identify and act on global trends. One of the central elements of his strategy has been his ability to understand central bank monetary policies and how these policies affect currency markets and financial assets in general.

In the vast history of financial markets, few events have resonated as deeply as the collapse of the British pound in 1992, an episode that not only redefined the economic landscape of the UK but also cemented Stanley Druckenmiller's reputation as one of the greatest global investment strategists. This event, known as "Black Wednesday," became a financial legend, demonstrating how a combination of sharp analysis, audacity, and perfect timing can move mountains—or, in this case, topple a national currency.

To understand the magnitude of the blow that Druckenmiller and his mentor, George Soros, another of the great investors in history, dealt to the Bank of England, it is essential first to understand the economic and political context of the time. In the early 1990s, the UK was part of the European Exchange Rate Mechanism (ERM), a system created to stabilize European currencies in preparation for the eventual creation of the euro. The ERM required member countries to keep their currencies within a fixed range of fluctuation relative to the German mark, which at that time was Europe's strongest currency.

The UK joined the ERM in 1990, at a time when its economy was weakened, suffering from high inflation and a prolonged recession. Despite these economic troubles, the British government, under Prime Minister John Major, decided to keep the pound in the ERM at a relatively high exchange rate compared to the German mark, in an attempt to demonstrate a commitment to stability and European integration.

However, this decision was controversial from the start. Many economists argued that the pound was overvalued, placing unsustainable pressure on the British economy. The high interest rates needed to defend the pound within the ERM were choking economic growth and increasing unemployment, causing growing discontent in the country.

Stanley Druckenmiller, who at that time was the chief manager of George Soros's Quantum Fund, began to analyze the UK's economic situation with a critical eye. Along with Soros, he concluded that the pound was severely overvalued and that the Bank of England would not have the resources or the capacity to defend its position in the ERM against the German mark, especially given the rising inflationary pressures and the underlying economic weakness of the UK.

Druckenmiller's reasoning was meticulous and calculated. He understood that the UK was trapped in a dilemma: to keep the pound within the ERM, the Bank of England would have to continue raising interest rates, which would further choke the economy, making it politically unsustainable to stay in the ERM. The other option would be to devalue the pound, which could revitalize the economy by making British exports more competitive, but at the cost of abandoning the ERM.

With this strategy in mind, Druckenmiller recommended to Soros that the Quantum Fund should bet massively against the pound. The idea was simple but powerful: if the UK could not keep the pound within the ERM, then the pound would fall, and they would make a fortune.

In September 1992, as the situation in the UK became increasingly precarious, Druckenmiller and Soros began to execute their plan. They started short-selling billions of pounds, using a combination of futures contracts and other financial instruments to bet against the British currency.

The scale of the bet was impressive and risky. With the Quantum Fund leading the charge, other investors began to follow suit, creating an avalanche of sales against the pound that put immense pressure on the Bank of England. The British government, desperate to defend the currency, raised interest rates to 15% and used billions of pounds from its reserves to buy the currency in the open market and support its value.

Ultimately, the pressure was too great for the Bank of England, which was forced to admit defeat. On September 16, 1992, a day that would go down in history as "Black Wednesday," the UK announced that it was withdrawing the pound from the ERM and would allow the currency to float freely in the markets. The pound immediately devalued, falling 15% against the German mark and 25% against the US dollar.

For Druckenmiller and Soros, Black Wednesday was a monumental victory. The devaluation of the pound generated approximately one billion dollars in profits for the Quantum Fund, a colossal sum that solidified the reputation of both investors as titans of the financial markets.

The collapse of the British pound had profound consequences for the UK. The decision to leave the ERM was seen as a national humiliation, and British monetary policy changed drastically in the following years. However, ironically, the devaluation of the pound also helped revitalize the UK economy, making exports more competitive and alleviating inflationary pressures, which eventually led to a period of sustained economic growth.

For Druckenmiller, this event was more than just a financial victory; it was a validation of his macroeconomic approach and his ability to identify and act on structural weaknesses in the global economy. The fall of the pound became a case study in business schools around the world and an example of the power investors can have over monetary policies when acting with conviction and precision.

After his success with Soros, Druckenmiller continued applying his focus on global trends to manage his own fund, Duquesne Capital, which he founded in 1981 and managed alongside Soros's fund until 2000. Druckenmiller's fund achieved an average annual return of 30% over three decades, never experiencing a losing year. This impressive track record positioned him as one of the most successful and respected investors in the world.

However, like all investors, Druckenmiller faced his worst moment during the dot-com crisis. By the late 1990s, the financial world was experiencing a radical shift. The technological revolution, driven by the rapid growth of the internet and technology-related companies, led to a surge in investments in this sector. Startups with scant revenue, and in some cases no clear business model, saw their valuations skyrocket to astronomical levels. The promise of the new digital economy led investors worldwide to rush into what seemed like a once-in-a-lifetime opportunity.

During this period, technology stocks inflated to unsustainable levels, and many investors, dazzled by the potential of these new technologies, began investing massively in them. The prevailing belief was that the future belonged to the internet and the companies driving it, and that any investment in this sector, regardless of the price, would be immensely profitable.

Stanley Druckenmiller, known for his approach based on deep macroeconomic analysis and his ability to foresee movements in global markets, understood that the market was being driven by irrational exuberance, a speculative fever that would inevitably lead to a correction.

Initially, Druckenmiller kept on the sidelines, aware of the dangers posed by a speculative bubble. He knew that the valuations of many of these technology companies were unsustainable and that, sooner or later, economic reality would prevail. However, as the bubble continued to expand, market pressure intensified. Investors around the world were making huge gains in a short period, and the temptation to participate in this boom became increasingly difficult to resist.

Despite his deep reservations and understanding of the underlying market dynamics, Druckenmiller eventually succumbed to the pressure. He decided to join the market frenzy, investing in technology stocks that, though inflated, were still perceived as an opportunity to profit in a rapidly growing environment. This decision marked a crucial moment in his career, as it meant deviating from his traditional approach based on macroeconomic analysis.

Druckenmiller knew he was taking a considerable risk, but he also understood that, in such an irrational market, staying on the sidelines could mean missing out on significant opportunities for returns. However, this decision, as he feared, soon began to backfire. As the bubble reached its peak, the first signs of a market collapse began to appear.

Druckenmiller hired Carson Levit, a renowned fund manager from Silicon Valley who didn't mind paying exorbitant prices for technology stocks. Although he sold some of the stocks in early 2000, Druckenmiller retained most of the tech stocks, saying that the Nasdaq was at an advanced stage of the bubble but still far from bursting.

The disagreements between Soros and Druckenmiller reached a climax over VeriSign, an internet security company that the fund bought for $50 per share the previous year and which had risen to $258 by the end of February. At Druckenmiller's urging, the funds doubled their bet on VeriSign to $600 million in early March. VeriSign's shares were at $240 when Druckenmiller decided to double the investment. However, when the Nasdaq fell, VeriSign's shares dropped to $135 in early April. Soros suggested reducing exposure, but a confident Druckenmiller responded, "No. This company is different from the rest of the dot-coms." But it wasn't, and VeriSign's shares fell to $96 in April.

At 7 a.m. on April 18, when the Quantum Fund had lost 21% for the year, Druckenmiller submitted his resignation, and the Soros Fund began the process of selling off most of its shares.

In these pages, you are witnessing how even the most successful investors face tough times, where their mistakes and failures led to some of the most challenging moments in their investment careers. I want to highlight this point, which should not be seen as a mere anecdote, as these difficulties, more often than not, instead of marking the end of their investment careers, became a turning point that made them better.

Druckenmiller, like other investors, managed to recover. By late 2007, Druckenmiller watched with growing concern the evolution of financial markets. The U.S. economy, driven by an unsustainable real estate boom and unprecedented credit expansion, was dangerously heading towards a crisis.

Druckenmiller understood that the market's irrational exuberance, fueled by a false sense of security, could not last indefinitely. Unlike the dot-com crisis, Druckenmiller began to adopt a defensive stance, preparing Duquesne Capital for the inevitable collapse. This stance included reducing exposure to risky assets and strengthening positions in assets that could benefit from or at least withstand a global recession.

Eventually, the warning signs became increasingly evident. The first signs of trouble in the mortgage market began to appear when "subprime" borrowers, those with poor credit histories, started defaulting on their payments in mass. Confidence in the global financial market began to waver, and the possibility of a systemic crisis became real.

Druckenmiller, who had anticipated this outcome, was prepared. As the subprime mortgage crisis spread and began to impact banks and other financial players, he took proactive measures. One strategy he employed was short-selling securities related to the real estate and financial sectors, betting that these assets would lose value as the crisis deepened. At the same time, he maintained investments in safer assets like U.S. Treasury bonds, which offered relative stability during times of uncertainty.

When the crisis reached its peak in 2008, with the collapse of Lehman Brothers and the failure of other major financial institutions, global markets plummeted. The decline was rapid and severe, wiping out trillions of dollars in market value and devastating the portfolios of countless investors. However, while many investment funds recorded catastrophic losses, Duquesne Capital, under Druckenmiller's leadership, not only avoided damage but also generated significant profits.

Druckenmiller achieved this by maintaining strict discipline and a clear focus on his macroeconomic analysis. This time, he avoided the traps that many other fund managers fell into by underestimating the severity of the crisis. One of his most astute decisions during this period was betting against the U.S. dollar, anticipating that the Federal Reserve, in an attempt to stabilize the economy, would inject large amounts of liquidity into the system, which would depress the value of the currency. This strategy proved successful, as the dollar indeed weakened in response to the Fed's expansive monetary policies.

The investor who had faltered during the dot-com crisis had learned his lesson perfectly. While the economy of much of the world was collapsing, Druckenmiller was making money with his various investment bets. The experience of the dot-com bubble left an indelible mark on Stanley Druckenmiller. It taught him that even the most experienced investors can be swept up by market euphoria and make decisions driven by external pressures rather than solid, well-founded analysis. In retrospect, the dot-com bubble was not just a challenge for Druckenmiller, but also a validation of his investment approach.

GERALDINE WEISS: THE DIVIDEND LADY

Geraldine Weiss, known as "The Dividend Lady," is an iconic figure in the investment world, recognized for her pioneering and successful approach to dividend-based stock selection. Her career, which challenged the conventions of her time, is an inspiring story of perseverance, innovation, and the ability to find a profitable niche in a male-dominated market. Throughout her life, Weiss not only earned the respect of her peers but also left a lasting legacy in dividend investing, an approach that remains relevant and valuable to today's investors.

Geraldine Weiss was born in 1926 in San Francisco, California, at a time when women were not encouraged to participate in the financial world. Inspired by her father, who instilled in her the value of financial education, Weiss showed an innate interest in business and investments. Despite the challenges faced by women at that time, Weiss decided she would pursue a career in finance.

Weiss attended the University of California, Berkeley, where she graduated with a degree in business administration. However, despite her education, she found that doors to the financial world were closed to her because of her gender. During the 1950s and 1960s, the financial industry was dominated by men, and it was almost unthinkable for a woman to establish herself as an investment expert.

Determined to overcome these barriers, Weiss began working at various financial firms, though she was often relegated to administrative or support tasks, far from decision-making roles. Frustrated by the lack of opportunities, Weiss decided to forge her own path in the investment world.

In 1966, she launched her investment newsletter, Investment Quality Trends (IQT), a publication dedicated to identifying high-quality stocks that offered sustainable long-term returns, known as "blue chips."

"Blue chips" are companies that have demonstrated their strength over time, weathering market ups and downs and consistently delivering value to their shareholders. These companies typically hold a leading position in their respective industries, offering products or services that are essential to everyday life. Additionally, they are known for their ability to pay regular dividends, making them attractive options for investors seeking stability and long-term profitability.

Investing in blue-chip companies is a common strategy for those looking for long-term capital growth combined with relatively low risk. Unlike high-growth stocks, which can be volatile, blue chips offer a more conservative approach that can protect investor capital during times of economic uncertainty.

Furthermore, the fact that many blue chips pay dividends makes these stocks appealing not only to those seeking growth, but also to those who wish to generate passive income. Dividends can be reinvested to purchase more shares, which, over time, can create a compounding effect, significantly increasing the value of the initial investment.

Typically, blue chips operate in sectors such as technology, consumer goods, energy, finance, and healthcare. Classic examples include companies like Apple, Microsoft, Coca-Cola, Johnson & Johnson, and ExxonMobil. These companies not only have a proven track record of financial performance but also possess a strong reputation and globally recognized brand, allowing them to maintain their dominant market position.

Geraldine Weiss's investment strategy focused on dividends, a form of passive income often overlooked by investors seeking quick gains in the stock market. Weiss understood that companies paying consistent and growing dividends not only generate recurring income but also tend to be more stable and secure in the long run. Instead of following the speculative trends of the market, Weiss adopted a quality and discipline-based approach.

Weiss based her strategy on the belief that dividends reflect a company's financial health. A company that can pay consistent dividends, even during economic downturns, demonstrates solid management and a sustainable business model. For Weiss, the relationship between dividends and stock price was a key indicator of whether a stock was undervalued or overvalued.

Her method involved identifying the "yield range," which is the range within which a company's dividend yield has historically fluctuated. When a stock's dividend yield was at the upper end of its historical range, Weiss considered it undervalued and a good time to buy. Conversely, when the dividend yield was at the lower end of its range, she considered the stock overvalued and a good time to sell.

This approach, known as "Dividend Yield Theory," became the cornerstone of her Investment Quality Trends newsletter. Over the years, this strategy proved to be incredibly effective, providing Weiss's subscribers with a clear and logical guide to investing in stocks.

High-yield stock selection was another key aspect of Geraldine Weiss's strategy. Not all dividend-paying companies are necessarily good investments. Weiss focused on companies that not only paid consistent dividends but also showed a history of dividend increases. She believed that companies with a stable policy of growing payments were more likely to be financially solid and well-managed.

For Weiss, it was crucial that selected companies had a history of at least 25 years of uninterrupted dividend payments, preferably with periodic increases. This criterion not only excluded younger and more volatile companies but also ensured that recommended investments were in companies that had demonstrated their ability to weather various economic conditions.

Some of the characteristics she looked for in stocks included a strong debt-to-equity ratio, efficient management, and a competitive advantage in their industry. Through her meticulous analysis, Weiss managed to identify companies that, although often overlooked by other investors, offered significant long-term capital growth potential along with stable dividend income.

Although not directly written by Geraldine Weiss, the book "Dividends Still Don't Lie: The Truth About Investing in Dividend Stocks," details the formula for her success. To select stocks with potential, Weiss established seven specific criteria that a company had to meet:

1. Dividend Yield Relative to Its History: If the current dividend yield is below its historical average, this could indicate an overvalued stock and vice versa.

2. Dividend Growth: Weiss looked for companies that had increased their dividends at a compound annual rate of at least 10% over the past 12 years. This sustained growth in dividends was a sign of financial strength and commitment to shareholders.

3. Book Value of the Stock: For Weiss, a stock priced at or less than twice the company's book value indicated a potential investment opportunity, suggesting that the stock was not overvalued relative to the company's assets.

4. Price-to-Earnings Ratio (P/E Ratio): She preferred stocks with a P/E ratio below 20, indicating that investors were not paying too much for the company's current earnings.

5. Dividend Payout Ratio: Weiss focused on companies that distributed less than 50% of their profits in dividends. This indicated that the company had room to reinvest in its own growth or to increase dividends in the future.

6. Debt Level: The company's debt should be equal to or less than 50% of its total market capitalization. A controlled debt level was crucial to ensure long-term financial stability.

7. Compliance with Blue Chip Criteria: Weiss applied six additional requirements to ensure the company was truly solid and reliable, including a history of dividend payments, a high credit rating from Standard & Poor's, a large market capitalization, a solid base of institutional investors, a continuous history of dividend payments for at least 25 years, and consistent earnings growth.

Moreover, as we have previously discussed, Weiss also developed a strategy to determine the optimal timing for buying and selling. She used a concept called the "Weiss Channel," which is based on the fluctuations in a stock's price within a range defined by the historical maximum and minimum dividend yields. According to this strategy, when a stock's price approached the historical maximum dividend yield, the stock was considered undervalued, and it was a good time to buy. Conversely, if the price was near the historical minimum dividend yield, the stock was considered overvalued, and it was the right time to sell.

However, Weiss warns us about certain aspects to watch for when investing in dividends.

Firstly, she recommends avoiding the pursuit of extremely high dividend yields, as they often indicate underlying problems within the company. Instead, she advises investors to focus on companies with moderate but growing yields, reflecting a healthy balance between paying dividends and reinvesting in the company's growth.

On the other hand, she argues that dividend investing requires patience, as the true value of these investments is realized over time. Dividends, when reinvested, can generate a compounding effect, allowing investors to steadily accumulate wealth over the years.

Finally, Weiss emphasizes that dividend investing is not a strategy for those seeking quick profits. Instead, it is an approach for investors who are willing to wait and let their investments grow over time. Patience, combined with dividend reinvestment, can yield impressive long-term results, even surpassing more aggressive strategies that rely on market speculation.

Throughout the book, Weiss provides numerous examples of how her dividend-based approach has resulted in significant successes for those who have followed it. One of the standout cases she highlights is Johnson & Johnson, a company that has consistently increased its dividends over decades. Investors who bought Johnson & Johnson stock and held it, reinvesting their dividends, saw their initial investment grow significantly over time. Such examples reinforce the idea that dividend investing is not only safe but also extremely profitable if discipline and patience are maintained.

Other examples such as Procter & Gamble and Coca-Cola were just a few of the cases that aligned with Weiss's criteria and, over the years, proved to be exceptionally profitable and secure investments.

Dividend investing has gained significant popularity in recent years, especially among those seeking financial independence, as dividends represent a stable and recurring source of passive income, making them a key component in the pursuit of financial freedom.

The main appeal of dividend investing lies in the predictability and tangibility of the income it generates. Unlike capital gains, which depend on selling stocks at a higher price than the purchase price, dividends provide a real cash flow that is deposited directly into the investor's account. This money, which can be used immediately or reinvested, offers a sense of security and steady progress towards financial independence.

However, although this strategy has its benefits, it is not necessarily the best option for everyone, especially for those with limited capital. One of the main challenges of dividend investing is that, for the income to be significant, considerable capital is required. For example, a 4% dividend yield on a $10,000 investment will generate only $400 per year, which may seem insufficient if the goal is to live off this type of passive income.

Additionally, another aspect that should not be overlooked is the tax burden associated with dividends. In many countries, dividends are subject to taxes, often at rates higher than long-term capital gains. This means that a significant portion of dividend income may be reduced by taxes, diminishing the net return for the investor. This taxation can complicate the path to financial independence, as it reduces the cash flow available for reinvestment or covering expenses.

Despite these limitations, dividends remain a powerful tool within a diversified investment strategy. For those with substantial capital, dividends can provide a relatively stable and predictable income stream. They offer a psychological advantage, as seeing money deposited regularly into an account can be motivating and reinforce commitment to a long-term investment plan. Moreover, as Geraldine Weiss said, "We all hope for capital gains, but what we can really count on is the dividend".

EPILOGUE

The journey through the pages of this book has taken us across a vast and diverse landscape of theories, strategies, and investment principles that have shaped the financial world as we know it today. From the fundamental basics underlying the importance of investing to the complex and sometimes esoteric methodologies employed by some of the most successful investors of all time, this text has aimed to capture the essence of what it means to be an investor in its broadest sense.

Investing is not merely an option but a necessity in the context of the modern world. The ever-present threat of inflation and loss of purchasing power, combined with the power of compound interest, makes investing a crucial tool for anyone aspiring to secure their financial future. We have learned that while saving is the first step toward building wealth, it is investing that truly drives that growth, allowing not only to protect capital against inflation but also to grow it exponentially over time.

Moreover, we explored various investment strategies, each with its own strengths, weaknesses, and optimal applications. From Value Investing, popularized by Benjamin Graham and refined by Warren Buffett, which teaches us to find value in seemingly irrational markets, to Growth Investing, which bets on the promising future of innovative companies.

Dividend investing offered us a different perspective, focusing on generating passive income and the power of reinvestment for compound growth. Here, the wisdom of figures like Geraldine Weiss showed us that dividends can be more than just periodic payments; they can be a cornerstone of a solid and reliable investment strategy.

Passive investing, ardently defended by John Bogle, demonstrated that sometimes less is more. In a world where the constant quest to beat the market can lead to unnecessary stress and hidden costs, the simplicity of an index fund can be the most sensible option for many investors.

In this book, we have sought to delve into the minds and methodologies of some of history's most influential investors. Each of these individuals not only achieved extraordinary results but also left a lasting legacy that continues to guide today's investors.

Throughout this book, we have tried to capture not only the techniques and strategies of great investors, but also the philosophy that drives them. Investing, as we have learned, is both an art and a science. It requires a combination of rigorous analysis, intuition, and, perhaps most importantly, a clear understanding of our own emotions and reactions to risk and uncertainty.

However, it is also important to recognize that we have not covered the entire spectrum of investment and fund management in this book. There are many other renowned investors and pioneers in the field who have greatly contributed to current investment knowledge and practices. Names like George Soros, with his theory of reflexivity and bold speculative investment style, or David Swensen, whose strategies in managing university endowments have revolutionized how institutional portfolios are managed, are just a few examples. The omission of these and other important investors is not meant to diminish their achievements but reflects the limitations of a single book to cover such a vast field.

As we close this chapter, it is clear that the world of investing is as dynamic as it is unpredictable. What has worked in the past will not always work in the future, and every investor must be willing to learn, adapt, and, above all, persevere. The lessons from the giants we have discussed here are timeless, but they must also be applied with a keen sense of the present and an eye towards what is to come.

Ultimately, this book has been an invitation to explore, learn, and, most importantly, to act. Investing is not just for experts or the lucky; it is an accessible tool for anyone willing to invest time and effort into understanding it. May this book be a step on your journey toward those goals, and may you find in investing not just a means to an end, but a passion that enriches your life in multiple ways.

Finally, I hope you have enjoyed this book, and as a self-published author, it would be greatly appreciated if, after purchasing this book through a platform, you could leave a positive review if you found it worthwhile. Thank you very much for reaching the last word of this book.

www.ingramcontent.com/pod-product-compliance
Lightning Source LLC
Chambersburg PA
CBHW070143230526
45471CB00002B/499